The Practical Canary Handbook

Breeding & Keeping Canaries

Written by Marie Miley-Russell

Photo on the front and back cover is a 7 week old American Singer canary chick.
Photograph by Marie Miley-Russell.

The American Singer canary model was adapted from the American Singer Club, Inc.
Constitution and used with permission.

All other graphics credit:
© 2005 Jupiter Images Corporation

Acknowledgments

Special thanks to:

- Jessie Durkin, Judy Snider, Alberta Riedel, Mike Grohman and Ed Medrano - for untold hours of patient tutoring.
- Jessie Durkin- for feedback and support.
- R. C. McDonald- better known as Robirda of www.robirda.com- for tutoring, advice, editorial assistance, and many kindnesses both large and small.
- Bill Miley, Karen West, and my own dear husband Kevin - for editing and support.
- Karen West- for answering myriad questions about various software programs at all hours.

Table of Contents

Introduction

When I began breeding canaries several years ago, I searched everywhere for information about canaries only to be frustrated- recently printed materials are too general and older materials tended to provide information that was arcane at best and incorrect at worst. Good quality books about canary breeding are difficult to locate as most of the best books ever written about the subject (such as Herman Osman's *Canary Breeding Tips and Tricks*) have been out of print for many years; the few more recently published books containing detailed information such as Linda Hogan's *Canary Tales* are self-published and readily available only to those with internet access.

Today the vast majority of information about canaries rests in the heads of experienced breeders and not in books or magazines. Obviously, this does little to assist the novice canary owner or breeder without access to a person with experience. I was fortunate enough to discover a specialty bird club which was extremely helpful in guiding me through the many problems I encountered early on. Several experienced members were very kind and generous, helping me frequently and without reservation. Without their assistance I would certainly have become discouraged.

To assist those without access to such help, I have gathered what information I have been able to learn about canaries into this book. My goal in writing was to try to pull together the bits and pieces of information from the many places in which the information now rests into a single source. *The Practical Canary Handbook* is not a comprehensive guide to canaries, but it should serve as a solid basis on which to begin learning.

I claim no special expertise; I have only compiled information from diverse sources such as written materials, discussions with fellow breeders and my own experiences. Hopefully, this book will provide some small assistance to both breeders and pet owners who desire to understand more about their canaries.

Yours in the Canary Fancy,

Marie Miley-Russell

General

The Canary, Past and Present

For more than four hundred years the canary has had a place in the homes of people who have valued them for their lively manner and cheerful sound. Several hundred years of careful selective breeding has led to such a diversity of shapes, sizes and colors that someone unfamiliar with the bird could easily be led to believe that the various breeds are different kinds of birds altogether and would certainly have difficulty believing that all these birds came from a rather nondescript little wild green canary.

Canaries have journeyed far to become the beautiful songsters they are today. While accounts differ as to the exact method by which they made their way to Europe, it is generally accepted that they originated as *Serinus c. canaria*, the wild green finch native to the Canary Islands, Madeira and the Azores west of Africa. In Europe, canaries were domesticated in the latter half of the fifteenth century and bred for nearly a hundred years in Portuguese and Spanish monasteries by cloistered monks who were careful to export only male birds in order to maintain a monopoly on the trade. Eventually- either by the smuggling of hens or by mistakes in sexing, breeders in Italy acquired pairs of birds and canariculture spread from there throughout Europe. It was very early in the domestication process that the yellow coloration which has come to be commonly associated with the canary first appeared.

Large scale canary breeding had its origins in the Tyrol Mountain region of Germany, where what began as a means for households to bring in supplemental income began to assume more importance when the local mining-based economy became depressed. By the 17th century, the canary breeding business was booming, with professional bird dealers journeying throughout Europe and even into Asia to sell canaries. The majority of these bird dealers purchased birds from individual breeders, traveling through Germany and Switzerland to buy young birds for resale elsewhere. Initially, these birds were for the most part colony bred with little attention paid to any particular characteristics. Eventually, a move developed toward the selection of canaries with especially quiet, pleasant and harmonious songs and lead to the creation of the Roller song breed in the Harz Mountains of Germany. The roller is a low- toned bird which sings with its beak closed. It has four basic tours or song passages- the hollow roll, knorre, flutes, and the hollow bell- and several supplementary tours which include water roll, glucke, and schockel. The roller's beautiful, deep hollow roll tour is one of its most recognizable tours. The quality of a roller is determined by its level of mastery of the individual tours and the overall quality with which it delivers them. Rollers are bred in nearly every color and some crested birds even exist.

Other areas of Europe developed their own types of song canaries. In 18th century western Belgium, breeders in the town of Malinois created the song canary called the Waterslager- which translated literally means "water beater" or "water striker"- after the notes it sings which sound like bubbling, plopping and rolling water. The Waterslager sings twelve different tours, including klokkende, bollende, rollende, staaltonen (or steel tone), fluiten (flutes), bellen (bell), belroll, tjokken, chorr, knorr and others. This canary sings with both open and closed beak and is a singer of moderate volume. The song of the Waterslager is wilder and more varied than the more refined song of the roller. The Waterslager standard states that birds must be yellow or white with minimal dark coloration of less than a centimeter in diameter.

In Spain, the song of the wild canary was preserved in the Spanish Timbrado- a bird which sings with an open beak in a higher pitch than either the roller or the waterslager. The song of this breed is best described as metallic. Notes sung by the Timbrado are described as continuous, in which notes are sung so quickly as to be impossible to individualize them; semi-continuous, in which the syllables of each tour can be detected but there is no clear pause between them; and discontinuous, in which there are very clear breaks between the expression of each syllable. In the Timbrado, three lines of birds exist- the floreados, which sing primarily discontinuous song with some semi-continuous notes; the classic, which sing primarily continuous notes with some discontinuous tours; and intermediate, which is somewhere between the floreado and classic types.

In Great Britain, canary breeders were more interested in the development of birds bred for type and posture than for song. British breeders were responsible for the creation of a large variety of breeds such as the Border, Fife, Norwich, Gloster, Yorkshire and other well known breeds.

Many of the present day breeds have been in existence for more than 200 years, but the past one hundred years has seen an explosion of development in the areas of color, conformation and song. Today canaries can be found in every color except true blue and purple. There are thin- and full-bodied canaries, canaries with frills and Beatles hairstyles, tiny ones and large ones . . . For those interested in song, there are canaries bred to sing softly and some bred to sing more loudly . . . Truly, there is a type of canary to suit everyone's tastes!

One of the most popular canary breeds in the United States is a colorbred bird called the red factor (actually a misnomer which refers to the gene the birds carry rather than to their coloration). Birds carrying the red factor gene come in a wide range of colors from the lightest pink through the darkest red. Other popular breeds are Glosters- birds bred for a particular body type and size which can be either crested or noncrested- and American Singers, a song breed developed in the United States. Spanish Timbradoes are also quite popular in many parts of the country.

While it is often difficult to state with certainty where and how a particular breed developed, breeds are often named after the place where the breed first took hold. For example, the Border canary is thought to have been developed along the border between England and Scotland and the American Singer was developed in the United States. Others such as lizard and frill canaries have been named for a distinctive plumage feature with the lizard possessing an unusual spangled pattern resembling the scales of a reptile and the frill being, well, frilly!

The so-called red canary is actually a genetically engineered canary. A strain of red-factor canaries is produced by the pairing of male Venezuelan hooded siskens (*Spinus cucullatus*) and canary hens over a period of five years. Depending on what type of canary is used to create a strain, the results can be very different. Today there are red rollers, borders, lizards, and many more. The red canary must be colorfed consistently to maintain peak coloration or it reverts to an orangish color with the molt.

The Gloster canary is a breed developed in England in the early part of the 20th century from the crossing of Border canaries and the crested roller. The breed produces both crested and noncrested- called consorts- birds (both are equally valuable as maintaining crest quality depends on pairing a crested bird to a consort mate). Though not as popular on the show bench as colorbred birds like the red canary, it is one of the most popular of the breeds bred for conformation and crested specimens are easily recognizable by their Beatles- style hairdo.

The American Singer is far and away the most common song type canary in the United States today. This breed is relatively inexpensive, free singing, and easy to breed and care for. It has become the perfect "pet bird" the original breeders were seeking when they developed the concept of crossing Border and Roller canaries in the 1930's to produce a medium-volume singer with great freedom, variety and melodiousness of song. The song of the American Singer- perhaps in imitation of the country of its origin- places the value of freedom above that of adherence to a formal song standard. Its song is not restricted to any particular style but can incorporate the best elements of all of the song breeds as long as the song is melodious, varied and freely given.

Song Type Canaries

Throughout history a wide variety of birds such as larks, linnets, thrushes, wrens, warblers, robins, finches and buntings have been kept for their song but from the earliest days canaries have been one of the favorite captive songbirds. Over the centuries, man has had profound effects on the song of the canary, manipulating and perfecting it until little remains of the original song of the wild canary of the Canary Islands.

A canary has a number of unique characteristics which make him an ideal songbird- he is easily kept and bred in captivity, is robust, and sings throughout the year unlike many other songbirds which sing only during certain times of the year. Canaries also possess a "vigor and variety" of song which makes them pleasant companions.

While it is true that all male canaries sing, there are particular breeds which have been developed strictly for song. The song of these breeds is longer and more melodious than that of canaries which have been bred for other qualities such as color or type.

One of the first countries to breed canaries on a large scale was Germany, which became so widely known for its canaries that by the 17th century canaries became known as German birds. While in other parts of Europe attention was devoted to breeding birds with particular physical characteristics, in Germany fanciers focused on the canary's song and German breeders soon became renowned for breeding birds with a quality of song not found in canaries elsewhere. Especially in the Harz Mountain area of Germany, where songbirds had long been kept, the number of canaries bred was staggering- a single town exported 12,000 male canaries in the year 1882 alone and a full three-quarters of the town's population was engaged in the canary business. By some reports, 150,000 male birds were exported annually from the Harz Mountains during the latter part of the 19th century.

The breed produced by the Harz Mountain breeders came to be called the Harz Roller or the German Roller. It was noted for its deep, hollow roll sung in the lower register. Quality roller song is sung with a closed beak. A song standard exists for this breed; birds are expected to sing certain tours such as hollow roll, bass roll, hollow bell and flute.

The Belgian Waterslager, developed in the Flanders area of Western Belgium, is another long-established song breed. The word waterslager means "water beater" and the birds were so named because their song contains a number of watery notes- sounds of dripping, bubbling and rolling water. Waterslager song is much more varied than the song of the Roller and also has a wider range, singing notes in both the low and high registers.

The Spanish Timbrado was recognized as a song breed in the 1970's by the C.O.M

(Confederation Orinithologogique Mondial or World Ornithological Confederation) and is popular in Spain, Latin America, and the United States. The name "Timbrado" comes from the Spanish word, "timbre," which means bell. Its song is closer to that of the wild canary with a higher pitch and a faster tempo than that of either the Roller or the Waterslager. The Timbrado has a loud song which closely resembles the music made by Spanish castanets.

The American Singer canary has not been recognized as a breed by the C.O.M. because it has no song standard. It remains, nonetheless, one of the most popular song breeds in the United States and Canada. The American Singer should display tremendous willingness to sing, be able to sing both low and high notes, and the song should possess no shrill or harsh notes. The song of the American Singer breed is allowed to change and evolve, becoming ever better and more free-flowing over time.

Another canary bred for song is the Russian Singer- also called the Russian canary- which is said to sing a type of song which is very close to that of native wild birds in Russia. Although it has a history of more than 300 years, it is virtually unknown in the United States at the present time. Originally developed from the German Roller, Russian breeders noticed the canary's ability to mimic the songs of different wild birds such as the trilling of the bunting. A variety of notes sung by other birds such as the sandpiper, the tit and the wood lark have also been incorporated into the Russian Singer's song. Birds are trained using a number of special musical instruments made for the purpose such as flutes and organs.

There is another canary kept for its song called the Persian singer, which originated in Arabic countries such as Iran. The song of the Persian singer is called "Moghoom," which means high rank. Information about this bird is difficult to locate, but it seems to be a variety of song rather than a particular breed of canary. The song is developed through separating twenty-four-day-old chicks which display physical characteristics such as a large head and chest and good, light-colored plumage. All chicks are placed in a completely soundproofed room in separate cages with an outstanding adult Persian singer tutor for a period of three months. After three months of tutoring, birds which are more successful at singing Moghoom are separated from those which have not adopted the preferred song. The birds are then kept for an additional three months in the same room with the tutor, but all cages are covered so that the birds cannot see each other. After the second three-month period, each bird is given one-on-one practice sessions with the tutor bird and only the birds most successful at copying the song of the tutor are kept. At one time very popular, the breed is in serious decline due to the demands of training birds and the importation of song breeds from the west.

American Singer Canaries

American Singer: The Roller-Border Cross

According to the constitution of the American Singer Club, Inc. (ASC), the breed was founded in Milton, Massachusetts in 1934 by a group of eight women breeders who sought to develop a canary bred for free, varied and harmonious song which was pleasing to the ear and neither too loud nor too harsh. The bird was to have a beautiful shape, tight feathering and please the average pet owner. This breed was to be created by following a plan that would result after five years of breeding in birds of 68 3/4% Roller ancestry and 31 1/4% Border ancestry. This breeding model is often referred to as simply "The Plan" by American Singer fanciers.

Birds are bred for song first- with freedom being the most important trait- and then for conformation. The song should be freely given, of medium volume, varied and melodious with no more than six chop notes in a row at any point in the song. Other factors in the song to consider are length of song, rendition and lack of repetition. Freedom is defined as the "willingness to sing, ease in starting and in performance of song."

Conformation is adherence to the breed standard as outlined in the ASC constitution. This model states that the individual bird is to measure 5 3/4 inches long measured from either the top of the head to the tip of the tail or from the tip of the beak to the tip of the tail. In terms of comparison to other canaries, this is a medium-sized bird. An American Singer should also have a lively, alert and fearless carriage. The bird should stand at an angle of 35 to 45 degrees from vertical and should not hoop the perch- stretch its head out and curve its body- when it sings as rollers do. In terms of its physical shape and condition, the body should generally be well proportioned and:

- the head should be rounded but not overly so, nor should it be flat with no dome;
- the beak should be medium-sized;
- eyes should be rounded and well-set;
- the neck should have neither too much nor too little indentation at the back of the neck between the base of the skull and shoulder (birds having too little are referred to as being snake-headed and those with too much are hollow- or thin-necked);
- the throat should have full expansion during song (failure to fully expand the throat while singing can be a sign of an anatomical defect or a singing hen);
- the shoulder should be pronounced;
- the back should be rounded, not too flat;
- the wings should be medium and should not be carried so that they cross each other at the tips;
- the breast should be rounded and full;

- little thigh should show;
- legs should be of medium length;
- the tail should be medium and close, not fish tailed (a very broad, rough tail with a V at the tip);
- feathering should be tight,
- and the bird should be in good condition- showing a "fullness of health, vigor and stamina."

This wording is not the exact phrasing of the American Singer standard as published in the constitution, but has been written to illustrate in plain terms to the novice how an American Singer should look. For the breed standard, reference should be made to the official ASC constitution.

Color is unimportant in the American Singer breed and should not be a consideration. While red American Singers are allowed on the show bench, birds which are colorfed will be disqualified from competition. Color feeding as defined by the ASC constitution is the "use of any food, vegetable dye, or color assist used before or during the molt to change the natural color of the specimen."

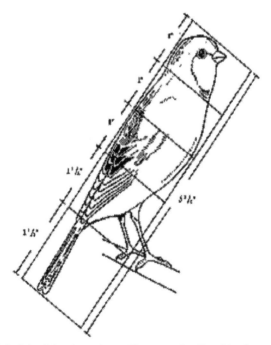

Model of the American Singer as Outlined in the Constitution of the ASC.

Freedom and the American Singer Canary

The American Singer canary was created for a single purpose: to produce a good song canary for pet owners. This raison d'etre is why the importance of freedom of song is the most important aspect of the American Singer song- pet owners love birds which sing frequently. Nothing makes a pet owner happier than a bird which begins singing as soon as his cover is removed in the morning and who is willing to sing regardless of the presence of strangers or activity in his environment.

In my experience with selling birds to "pet people"- as breeders refer to those seeking to purchase pets rather than breeding stock- a bird which sings freely will sell before other birds whose song may be far superior. The need to breed birds with a great deal of freedom for the pet market dovetails neatly with the need for those who exhibit to produce birds with a lot of freedom because no matter how beautifully a bird sings in the show, if he does not sing his ten songs during the ten-minute freedom period he will have a very hard time placing in the top six on the show bench.

The drive to sing comes from within a bird- it is the single thing which cannot be changed in a bird's song. No amount of tutoring or show training will ever teach a bird to sing more often. I learned this the hard way after I lost several breeding seasons working with a line of wonderful sounding birds which lacked freedom. The entire line was based on a male I came to call "the Stealth Singer." This bird had a beautiful rich tone that was a joy to hear and near-perfect conformation, but he refused to sing when I was in the room. If I hid around a corner, he would sing- when I peeked, he would close his beak! I trained that bird better than I have ever trained another canary- he was carted all over the house, driven everywhere and taken to visit everyone I visited. When he arrived at a show, he would sing if no one was looking at him but shut his beak as soon as anyone's head turned toward him. At five different shows in his first year, he spent the entire time on the show bench hopping from one perch to the other. In the holding room I received loads of compliments on his wonderful song, however!

As the saying goes, if I had known then what I know now I would have considered him the dead end that he was. Being a complete novice, I decided to try to breed him into a line of birds with loads of freedom in hopes of producing babies who sang more often. I ended up with a couple dozen birds that had exceptional conformation but lacked freedom just like their father- though in all fairness they would actually sing if I looked at them, which was an improvement.

As I dearly loved the Stealth Singer's song, I didn't give up- the following year I bred him to hens from a line of birds which carried even more freedom than the one from the previous year and I bred his daughters to males which sang nearly every waking moment . . . I ended up with lots of babies which, while beautiful birds and nice singers, refused to sing at the shows. I suppose that if I had continued this for several more years, I would have ended up with freer singing birds, but the song of the offspring became less and less like the Stealth Singer's every generation so it seemed an exercise in futility to continue any farther with the line. Based on this experience, I decided to radically change my breeding philosophy. I ruthlessly eliminated from my birdroom any bird which did not exhibit great freedom- as long as the bird had no unpleasant harshness or truly objectionable notes, the bird stayed as long as it was willing to sing all the time. Even the Stealth Singer was sold. I bred only the freest- singing birds I could locate. The chicks produced from that season's breeding were sorted based on freedom first- if a bird didn't show a great deal of freedom it was eliminated from my breeding program. Currently at seven months of age, the offspring of these chicks are showing much more freedom than I have ever seen in my birdroom- babies began singing before they were removed to weaning cages, sang all the way through the molt and are willing to sing even when I am standing in the walk in flight inches away from them and looking at them. All indications are that my efforts to breed birds with a great deal of freedom are beginning to pay off.

Lack of freedom is an inherited trait which can be an insurmountable challenge to show training. Often novices are told that they need to work more on show training their birds when careful investigation would show that it is the birds themselves which need to be worked on rather than their level of training. Birds can be bred who require little in the way of training- all that they require is a little time to become familiar with the new cage and its setup and some basic exposure to different experiences and they are ready for the show bench. The average bird will require more than this to become ready for the shows but there is little reason why a line cannot be developed to require a minimal amount of training. Not only would this be of benefit to the exhibitor, but also to the breeder seeking to sell surplus birds to pet owners.

How to Buy an American Singer Canary

DO:

- <u>Your research before buying a bird</u>. Make sure you know what breed you are interested in, what you should look for in a canary in general and in one of your preferred breed, the typical price range of the breed, and what the general care requirements will be.

- <u>Buy from breeders who also exhibit.</u> An exhibitor keeps his stock so that they will be in good condition to show and he also tends to have better quality stock than the ordinary breeder of common canaries. Additionally, a breeder who exhibits is more likely to be knowledgeable about the breeds he owns.

- <u>Buy from reputable breeders.</u> Breeders are not all honest, unfortunately. Some knowingly sell novices inferior quality stock. While this does not tend to be a common problem with American Singer breeders, I have heard many horror stories about other types of canaries. Knowing what you need to look for in a bird can help you avoid many problems.

- <u>Make sure you are buying real American Singer canaries</u>. Many breeders use the term American Singer for any kind of canary that sings and is born in America, but unless it has a closed leg band registered to a member of the national American Singer Club, the bird could be anything.

- <u>Be patient.</u> Most breeders are happy to place you on a waiting list and contact you when the birds are ready for new homes. Often this is one of the best ways to get a quality bird from a serious breeder. It is preferable to wait a few months for a good bird than to impulsively buy a canary simply because it's available immediately.

- <u>Join a local American Singer chapter and work at the shows.</u> Fellow club members are more likely to sell better stock to hard-working novices who look like they will stick around for some time. Working at the shows also helps a novice gain invaluable experience and make contacts.

- <u>Buy young breeding stock, if possible</u>. Be sure to ask about the parent's backgrounds and whether or not they come from good feeding lines. If possible, ask to listen to a hen's father to get an idea of what sound she carries.

- <u>Be respectful of the breeder's time</u>. Most breeders don't mind taking extra time with a novice who is eager to learn more about the birds, but they do have lives. Be sure to ask if the breeder will have time to speak with you when you come to pick up your bird and if not, if there would be a better time to arrange to meet with him. Be on time if at all possible, but call if you will be late or need to cancel an appointment.

- <u>Realize that breeders will not sell their best breeding stock.</u> Top quality stock represents an enormous investment of time, money, and knowledge. For a large majority of breeders who exhibit, there are certain birds which will not be sold for any amount of money as they represent the culmination of many years of hard work. It is sometimes possible, however, to purchase a related bird which is not needed for the breeder's program.

- <u>Offer to pay cash</u>. Most breeders are leery of accepting checks from people they don't know well.

DON'T

- <u>Buy birds until after the baby molt.</u> There are always breeders willing to sell young, unsexed birds cheaply. Most of the time these "unsexed" birds have in fact been sexed- as hens! By selling these birds as unsexed, the breeder tacks on an extra $10 or so because it *might* be a male and leaves the buyer believing he got a bargain.

  Additionally, the molt is a very stressful time in a bird's life and some babies do not survive it- why take the chance? If a breeder who claims to be an exhibitor is selling birds this young, one needs to ask oneself why. No serious exhibitor will sell stock before having a good idea about what the bird is and what kind of song he has. Generally, this would not be until fall.

- <u>Buy molting birds.</u> Molting birds are under a tremendous amount of physical stress. Moving them at this time can kill them- sometimes within hours. One unscrupulous bird dealer who I have seen at a number of bird fairs selling molting birds has dead birds in his cages nearly every time he arrives- yet he sells out his stock more often than not!

- <u>Buy nesting birds.</u> One would think this would go without saying, but I've seen it happen at a bird fair. The seller stated that the pair of canaries had given her "several nests of babies already this year" and indicated that the eggs were a bonus . . . While loading the cage into her car, the buyer jolted the nest and the eggs were broken. The seller's response was "don't worry- they'll have more!" More than likely the hen would have abandoned the nest even had the eggs survived (and been fertile). No reputable breeder will sell nesting birds. Don't walk away from these "bargains"- run!

- <u>Buy a male canary unless you hear it sing.</u> If you buy a canary without hearing it sing, you should only do so from a breeder you *have the utmost trust in* because you have purchased the proverbial "pig in a poke." The bird could be a hen, it could lack freedom and sing rarely, it could be ill or have a terrible song- or it could simply not be show trained. But how to tell? Especially when buying breeding stock, always listen to the bird before buying it!

- <u>Purchase birds just because they are from a particular breeder</u>. Even the best breeders produce mediocre birds. Once again, make sure you listen to the male! With hens the issue is more difficult as you cannot tell what song she carries, but you can and should evaluate her conformation. If possible, ask to listen to her father and brothers.

- <u>Buy a bird based on color.</u> American Singers are bred for song and color should not be a consideration. I have seen many buyers walk away from wonderful birds because they wanted a yellow canary. If you are breeding with the intention of showing, it is best to be blind to color and buy stock for song and conformation because judges will not be moved by the color of the birds, only their songs.

- <u>Be afraid to leave empty-handed.</u> Many buyers seem to think that they must buy a bird- even if they don't care for it or are bothered by the conditions the birds are kept in. If in any doubt, leave the bird where he is!

Basic Canary Care

What kind of housing should I provide for my single canary?

Canaries should be housed in cages with no greater than 5/8 inch bar spacing; ½ inch is standard. Any wider bar spacing can allow a bird to stick his head through the bars and strangle itself.

Despite the fact that pet bird cage manufacturers produce great numbers of tall, round, highly ornamented cages, what a canary really needs is a simple rectangular cage which is longer than it is tall to provide room to fly back and forth. Some height is beneficial since a bird that has to fly from a high perch down to the floor of its cage and back up is exercising some of the same muscles it uses to sing.

Locating a good cage in a pet store is often difficult- the majority of cages sold there are simply inappropriate and more hassle than they are worth. Most of my customers who have purchased cages in pet stores tell me that they have had to buy a more suitable cage within a few months, so it is best to simply buy a good cage in the beginning and save the money.

The only cage I recommend for canaries is a flight cage- this is a rectangular cage that provides plenty of space for flying back and forth as well as allowing for up and down flight. It has room for placing perches at different heights, is easy to clean, and allows for full viewing of the bird. Wooden cages or highly decorative cages are hard to clean and provide mites and other parasites space to hide and breed. Metal or plastic coated metal is fine- it's easy to clean and sterilize. Floor grills are not necessary and add to clean up work. Many flight cages are made with an unremovable floor grill- removing it makes the entire cage unstable. Unremovable grills can be covered with newspaper. As for cage size, the general rule of thumb is the larger the better unless birds will be let out of the cage daily for exercise.

The best- and most inexpensive- material to use for covering the cage floor is newspaper. Other items such as ground corncob, wood shavings, etc. harbor parasites, bacteria, and can grow moldy if they become wet. It is difficult to clean fresh food out of the cage if one uses materials such as wood shavings- canaries often scatter or carry food to other parts of the cage and may become ill from eating spoiled tidbits they locate in the bedding. Besides the tendency of the material to scatter in the breeze created by birds in flight, some birds develop a habit of gathering this material up and soaking it in their water dish as well which is unsanitary. Newspaper can be laid down in a single layer and rolled up, thrown out and replaced in a few seconds on a daily or every other day basis.

Sunlight is important to a bird's health. Place the cage in a bright location with a portion of the cage out of direct sunlight so the bird can take shelter and avoid overheating. If natural sunshine is not available, a full-spectrum light should be used to ensure that your bird receives an adequate amount of light.

Fresh air is wonderful, but keep your pet out of hot or cold drafts including those created by fans, heat and air conditioning vents. Sometimes a bird can get a draft from an unexpected source- such as when air from a fan directed away from his cage bounces off of a wall or other object and is redirected back at the cage. The common wisdom is that if the flame of a candle flickers near his cage, it is probably too drafty for your bird. This said, I believe that a certain amount of airflow is needed and that the gentle breeze from a window will not harm a canary as long as he is able to move out of it if he desires (a cloth can be placed over one end of the cage to block the breeze) and the breeze is not either extremely colder or hotter than the overall temperature of the room. Certainly, a breeze from an air conditioning or furnace vent would not be good.

Generally, a canary will be comfortable at the same room temperature people are- 65 to 70 degrees. Be careful if the temperature becomes too high as this can stimulate your bird into an unseasonable molt.

What accessories does my bird require?

A bird needs good, clean perching- except for when your bird is in flight, he will stand on his feet his entire life. Plain wooden perches are by far the best for foot health. *Do not use sandpaper perch or cage floor covers*- they are extremely abrasive to the pads of the feet and the toes and can cause sores. Using a single sandy perch is okay as long as it is not the highest perch in the cage- birds generally sleep or "roost" on the highest perch and would spend too much time on the rough surface.

Canaries need 3/8 to 3/4 inch perches- wide enough that their toes do not completely wrap around the perch. It is important that the bird has perches of different diameters available as well so his feet are properly exercised. Pet stores sell so-called "Wild Walk" perches that have varying widths and work well. If you cannot locate that type of perch, simply vary the sizes of perches so he always has a couple of different width perches in the cage.

Having extra sets of perches is important- this allows for thorough cleaning and sterilizing of perches. Perches should always be completely dried before placing them back in the cage- cold, damp perching is very bad for bird feet as well as unpleasant for your bird! Simply scraping perches off is not sufficient- they need to be washed in a mild cleanser and sterilized with either a short soak in a bleach/water solution or laid out in the sunshine for several hours.

In a pinch, perches which have no metal parts may be dried in a microwave oven for a very short period- only a few seconds are usually sufficient. Be careful- wooden perches will catch fire and burn quickly. Also, when microwaving cotton perches to which plastic connectors are attached with glue you must be aware that the glue will melt if left in the microwave for too long. I have found that this is the best option for drying cotton rope perches as it prevents the perch from developing a musty odor after washing. Place the perch inside the microwave on a piece of paper toweling, microwave for 10-15 seconds depending on the strength of your microwave and then remove from the oven (once again, be careful- the perch <u>will</u> steam and could burn you). Allow the perch to cool and if it still feels damp, microwave it again for 10-15 seconds- repeat the process until the perch is completely dry. I cannot stress enough the importance of being careful when handling the hot perches or in paying very close attention while heating them! This procedure has the added benefit of sterilizing the perches while it dries them.

Feeding dishes should be shallow- canaries are not parrots and will not dig through their dishes looking for food. Most of the seed cups that are supplied with cages are inappropriate- one of the best dishes is a glazed clay saucer sold for use under clay pots. Make sure to use only those which are glazed inside- plain clay saucers hold bacteria and cannot be properly sterilized. Shallow glass ashtrays work as well! Whatever you use, the dishes need to be clean so having several extra sets is a must. Finger treat cups which slide between the cage bars are wonderful for providing song food and other foods; these can be purchased for less than 25 cents at online stores or at bird shows. Occasionally pet stores will stock finger treat cups as well.

Your bird will need fresh, clean water every day- birds will die within 36 hours without access to water. Bird bottles are excellent and most birds learn to drink from them quickly. They keep water clean and free from food particles and droppings which can contaminate your bird's drinking water. (These must be watched, however, as on occasion they quit working and leave your bird without water.) Fresh water should still be provided every day even if using a bird bottle. I have found the plastic gerbil/hamster type of water bottle to be considerably less expensive and more readily available than bottles marketed for birds. These are suitable for canaries and finches, but larger birds will destroy them- they require glass bottles. If using a water bottle with a bird for the first time, be sure to provide an alternative water source until it becomes apparent that the bird has learned how to drink from it. In my experience, they do learn fairly quickly- especially when placed with other birds who are accustomed to water bottles so that they can learn from watching others drink from the bottle. If using an open water dish, replace it whenever the water becomes dirty and refill it if your bird empties it by bathing in it. Having extra water dishes on hand is also a must!

Your canary should have a cuttlebone available at all times to provide opportunity to keep his beak worn down and to provide calcium. Not all birds will use a cuttlebone, but it should be available- most especially during the molting period and breeding season as birds require extra calcium during these times.

If your bird's cage will be placed in an area where he will be exposed to artificial lighting, you will need a cage cover. Canary hormones are regulated by daylight length and too many hours of light can cause an unseasonable molt. Maintaining a regular schedule for him will be easier if you can cover his cage.

Some canaries enjoy swings and other toys. Do not provide your bird with a mirror; canaries can become very aggressive toward a mirror as they view their image as a rival. Other canaries will refuse to sing in the presence of a mirror. Small preening-type toys are generally favorites, but every bird is an individual so experiment and see what your bird prefers!

What should I feed my bird?

A good quality, FRESH vitamized seed mix blended especially for canaries is essential and should be before the birds at all times. A good basic seed mix should be about 80% canary seed and 20% rapeseed (also called canola seed).

Do not purchase finch seed or canary/finch seed blends as these contain too much millet and other high fat, high energy seeds which finches require but canaries do not. If you are located in an area where it is difficult to locate good fresh seed consider buying a larger quantity of feed over the internet and storing the surplus in plastic freezer bags in your freezer. It will stay fresh for a very long time and you can save on shipping costs. (Be sure to allow the seed to return to room temperature in an *open* container to prevent moisture buildup inside the package which can lead to the feed becoming moldy.)

Song food or other treat seed should be provided only a couple of times per week and in small quantities as it is high in fat, calories and protein and too much can cause your bird to become obese and develop health problems. Petamine (adult bird formula) is a supplement which can be given to the birds a few times a week as well. This can generally be located in pet stores. Baked, finely crushed eggshells can be provided to supply calcium in addition to cuttlebone.

Several brands of pellets are available such as Zupreem, Pretty Bird, Harrison's and many others. Some of these pellets are advertised as a complete diet to be used in place of seed, but I find that they are better used as an addition to their daily seed. Some people mix pellets in with the daily seed mixture but I serve them to my birds in a finger treat cup- when they eat all the pellets they get a refill. This way they have access to pellets every day and there is less waste.

Fresh fruits and vegetables are essential. Canaries enjoy apple, orange, cantaloupe, grated carrots, broccoli, endive, dandelion greens (chemical free), kale, cucumbers and many other kinds of fruits and vegetables. Fresh foods should be given in moderation as too much can cause loose stools and lettuces (other than romaine) should not be given to birds at all, as it has very little nutritive value. Make sure to clean leftover fresh food out of your bird's cage at the end of the day to ensure that they do not eat spoiled food!

The debate over grit is ongoing. On the advice of several experienced breeders, I have never provided grit to my canaries; I have yet to see a bird suffer for lack of it. I have, however, heard of babies killed when their mothers fed them mineral grit- the grit built up in their guts and blocked their intestines (as discovered during a necropsy), leading to the death of entire nests of babies. For this reason, I would recommend against providing any kind of grit to breeding canaries.

Vitamins should not be mixed in water- at best, this is an ineffective method of vitamin administration (studies have shown that availability of vitamins given in water drops substantially after the first half hour) and at worst, it is potentially dangerous as the vitamin/water mixture forms the perfect environment for bacteria to grow. Excellent avian vitamin supplements such as Prime and others are available at most pet stores or online and can be served sprinkled on top of fresh food. Be sure to follow the manufacturer's directions to avoid overdosing! If providing a vitamized seed one should not give supplemental vitamins.

Seed must be blown off daily to remove empty husks- many canaries have starved to death when their seed dish appeared full!

Clean, fresh water must be present at all times. Be careful with using well water as some wells can be contaminated with bacteria and chemicals which, while not posing a problem for people or larger animals, can sicken canaries. If you have any doubt about the quality of your tap water, provide bottled water.

How often should I clean my bird's cage?

The simple answer is when it's dirty! Perches should be changed at least every other day- sooner if there is visible soiling. Food dishes should be clean and free from all soil and water dishes should be changed *daily*. I have yet to meet the person who would be happy to drink from the same dirty glass for a week or more- I'm sure your bird won't be either!

Cage papers need to be changed regularly. Remember, your bird is hopping through his droppings and carrying this up to his perches- cleaner papers result in cleaner perches.

Cages should be cleaned regularly- how often depends on the size of your cage. Larger cages require less frequent washing than small cages, which tend to become dirty much quicker. In my birdroom, all cages are taken outside for power washing once a month and allowed to dry in the sunshine. In colder weather, cages are wiped down as needed.

17

Can I keep several canaries together?

It depends. Male canaries should be housed separately. Two males caged together WILL fight-sometimes until one is killed or both are injured badly. Once in a while two males seem to work out an arrangement and do manage to live together in relative peace but in almost all of these cases, one of the males stops singing. Males caged separately seem to enjoy the presence of each other and encourage each other to sing more often, though, so having another bird for companionship is beneficial.

Female canaries can be caged together throughout the year, though once again they do have their own personalities and some get along better than others.

Males and females should NOT be kept together at any time except during the breeding season and during the molting period (BOTH must be in full molt, however). Males can chase a hen to death trying to mate with her and hens can be pushed into laying eggs when they are not in condition to do so, which can lead to egg binding and death.

What if my male canary stops singing or my new canary doesn't sing?

Healthy male canaries sing because their hormones- especially testosterone- tell them to! They sing to attract a mate, to declare territory and sometimes simply for their own pleasure. The song announces to other canaries that the singer is healthy and strong.

If for some reason your bird's testosterone level drops, he will sing less frequently or quit altogether. This happens every year during the molting period, when a bird loses and replaces all of his feathers. The majority of male birds will not sing during the molt, which lasts between six and eight weeks. Some older males also experience declining testosterone levels and sing less frequently than when they were younger.

Singing is also a sign of health- weak, stressed, or ill birds will not sing.

Sometimes a bird will quit singing due to environmental reasons such as being placed with a hen (after all, why should he sing to attract a mate when he has one?), having a mirror (he views the other canary as a mate), being frightened, being placed in a dimly lit or too quiet setting, or sometimes just because he doesn't care for his cage location. (Birds have preferences, too!)

If your bird stops singing when he has previously, appears to be in good health and is not molting, then check and see if there is anything different in his environment that may have upset him. Sometimes you have to put yourself in your bird's place- can he see out a window where hawks or a neighbor's cat can be seen? Have you introduced a new pet or member of the family? Given him a new toy? A little problem solving will often provide the answer.

A new bird should sing soon after bringing him home- within a couple of weeks at least. If your bird never sings at all, it is possible that it is a female- though some male birds do lack freedom (the drive to sing) and only sing infrequently.

Remember that all birds are individuals and what makes one happy could bother another. Many canary buyers insist that because their previous canary always had a mirror and sang anyway, their new one should do the same. Not so!

One of the biggest environmental problems I have seen is when a canary is taken from an aviary setting- which is noisy and boisterous- and placed in a very quiet, single- canary home. This is terrifying for the bird and he will need a longer period of adjustment as well as some low background noise- a television, radio or other sound. Eventually, the bird should sing but will probably not sing as frequently as one with more stimulation.

There are feathers all over the place- what is going on?

Healthy birds molt once per year, usually in the summer when the length of the days is longer and temperatures are warmer. This process generally lasts six to eight weeks and is a very stressful time for your bird as his body is working very hard to replace all the worn out feathers he has been wearing (and using) for the past year. Molting generally begins on the upper body and works its way over the body gradually so the bird is never entirely without feathers or the ability to fly. The last place to molt is the head- so when pin feathers (new feathers emerging from the skin which are still encased in the sheath in which they develop which look like tiny white pins) appear on your birds head, the molt is almost over.

Birds during this period need extra attention regarding their nutrition- good nutrition produces good quality feathers!

Feathers are largely protein and so a molting bird's protein needs are higher. A small amount of boiled egg is helpful, although care should be taken to not leave egg in the cage for longer than thirty minutes to avoid the risk of food poisoning. A high quality dry commercial molting/nestling food such as Petamine should be provided as well. Good nutritional supplements to provide at this time are spirulina and bee pollen, which provide a range of benefits including additional protein and carotenoids (which are used by the body to produce coloring in the feathers).

Providing a little extra fat in the diet at this time is beneficial- oily seeds such as flax will help add luster to the new plumage. Song food can be provided every other day during this time. Carrots, sweet potatoes and beets are excellent sources of beta carotene which will help your bird to develop the pigmentation to provide deeper, richer feather coloration- yellow birds will be a richer yellow and green birds will be a richer green (within the limits of their genetics, of course).

An excellent product for providing a boost during the molt is Feather-Up available from www.birds2grow.com. It contains multivitamins, amino acids, and protein.

Birds should be provided with regular cold water baths at all times of the year, but especially during the molt. Bathing assists in softening the feather sheaths and makes it easier for the feathers to expand. A small amount of Listerine or apple cider vinegar in your bird's bath water will give your bird's feathers a lustrous sheen and assist in fighting mites. Morning baths are best- never let a bird go to sleep wet!

Birds who molt more than once a year or whose molt continues for longer than ten weeks may be malnourished or ill. Make sure that your bird is not exposed to hot or cold drafts, high temperatures or other environmental factors which can trigger a molt as well.

How often should my bird's nails be trimmed and how should I do it?

Canary nails only need to be trimmed once or twice a year depending on how quickly your individual bird's nails grow. Nails which grow too quickly can be an indicator of poor health or improper diet.

Canary nails can easily be trimmed using a pair of fingernail clippers. If your bird has light-colored toenails hold your bird's toes up to the light and locate the thin red line- this is the vein. Cut the nail carefully below this point to avoid causing bleeding. If your bird has dark colored nails you will not be able to see the vein- in this case, just tip the nails by cutting only a small bit off the end.

Be sure to have something on hand to stop bleeding if you happen to cut too closely- a commercial styptic powder or in a pinch, corn starch. Birds can easily bleed to death from loss of blood.

What if my bird refuses to bathe?

Birds, like people, have personal preferences about bathing. Some birds- especially males- simply refuse a regular bath while other birds empty out their water cups several times a day taking baths. Some birds are so insistent on bathing they will try to take showers in their water bottles if not provided with a dish of water every day!

Birds may be spooked by the bathing dish. Bathing dishes made for small birds with a mirror on the bottom terrify some canaries while others don't seem to mind at all. A bird unused to a bird bath which hangs on the outside of a cage will often refuse to enter it for weeks or months even though it is hung on the cage regularly. Birds are naturally suspicious of anything new in their environments, but given enough time they will generally adapt. Whatever the cause, it is

not a reason for alarm. Nearly all birds will bathe at one time or another.

A clean spray bottle filled with a tablespoon of Listerine and warm water can be used to mist birds which refuse all inducements to bathe. Gently spray a fine mist over the bird's cage- opening the cage and spraying right at the birds will terrify them. Be sure to remove food and water dishes before misting the birds in their cages and allow sufficient drying time so birds do not go to sleep with wet feathers. Many birds come to enjoy this and I have converted several "non-bathers" by misting them every day.

Can canaries be kept together with other kinds of birds?

The answer to this is a qualified "yes." Canaries may be kept successfully with certain kinds of finches such as society or zebra finches. Sometimes the higher-strung finches seem to get on the mellower canary's nerves, however. And communal housing will affect both the quality and quantity of the canary's song- a canary who gets jostled around by energetic finches will be frequently interrupted and he may develop the bad habit of breaking off his song. Additionally, his song will be corrupted by the finch sounds he hears every day. Finches also require a higher fat content in their diets and higher caloric intakes than do canaries. For this reason, canaries housed with finches may become fat.

Canaries should never be housed with hook bills of any kind- canaries usually end up with toes bitten off if they are fortunate and seriously injured or dead if they are not. Besides the danger to the canary kept in this situation, the two types of birds have very different dietary requirements.

How long will my canary live?

This is highly variable. In general, pet canaries live longer than breeders due to the strain of raising babies.

A pet canary can live anywhere between 8-10 years on average, although I have had pet owners who have had birds live as long as 18 years- and sang right to the end of their lives! This is certainly the exception rather than the norm, however.

Canaries that have been used for breeding usually live about 5 years. Again, this is a generalization as many breeders have certainly had birds which lived and successfully bred much longer than this. Birds may still breed at five years and older, but fertility does tend to decline. Their ability to survive the rigors of breeding season and the following molt is also reduced.

Dangerous Foods for Canaries
<ul><li>Moldy, spoiled and poor grade foods.</li><li>Avocado- this is very toxic to birds.</li><li>Coffee and coffee beans.</li><li>Rhubarb leaves- whether raw or cooked, the level of oxalic acid in the leaves is poisonous.</li><li>The green parts of tomato plants.</li><li>Potato shoots.</li><li>The green parts of potato plants.</li><li>Cat or dog food- these can contain bacteria.</li><li>Foods high in oxalic acid should be fed sparingly as oxalic acid can damage the kidneys and bind nutrients such as calcium, preventing proper absorption. These foods include vegetables such as spinach, beets and beet leaves, purslane, chard, parsley, chives, cassava and amaranth.</li><li>Salty foods.</li><li>Chocolate.</li><li>Alcohol- this can be lethal even in very small doses.</li><li>Yeast- uncooked.</li></ul>

Feeding

Seeds and Supplements- Feeding, Nutrition and Uses

All seeds and supplements are listed with the name used most commonly in the United States first, followed by the British term where applicable. I have included more detailed nutritional analysis where it could be located.

All seed and supplements fed should be clean and there should be little foreign matter such as branches, stems and hulls. Seeds with small holes in them indicate infestation by seed moths. Dusty seed can be caused by age, heat exposure and poor storage conditions. An easy test for freshness of seed is sprouting. Cover a dish with dampened paper towel, spread a single layer of seeds on the towel and keep the seeds moist by placing the dish inside a plastic bag and wetting as necessary. Good quality fresh seed should sprout quickly- within a day or two- and at least 75% of the seed should be sprouted within four days. If less than 75% of the seed sprouts, the seed is either too old or it is spoiled.

It is best to purchase seed in sealed bags and in quantities that can be used within six weeks. If a freezer is available, larger quantities can be purchased and stored in large sealable plastic bags. When removing seed from the freezer, be sure to allow it to thaw in open containers to prevent seed from becoming moldy! All unfrozen seed should be stored in cool, dry conditions in covered containers such as plastic pails or garbage cans with lids.

Seed moths are best contained by freezing seed for 48-72 hours before using. The moths and their larvae are not harmful to the birds if eaten, however.

The nutritional level of all seeds and supplements is largely dependent on environmental growing conditions- variables such as soil fertility, weather conditions, etc. have an enormous impact on food, therefore any nutritional information should only be used as a rough guide. An excellent example of this is bee pollen- depending on what bee colonies have fed on, protein content can be as low as 9% or as high as 37%.

Some of these items could also be included in the chapter on herbs and natural supplements. Those which are used most commonly are included here while herbs and natural supplements used less often are included in the next chapter.

As I researched many of these items I was surprised to discover that many of them have been noted for centuries for their medicinal uses, especially for easing digestive complaints. Canary breeders have long been known for experimentation and close observation of their birds-perhaps this is one reason why these seeds have come to be included in the canary's diet.

Canary Seed
- A major component of canary foods since the earliest days of canariculture, it is a grass plant. Originally native to the Mediterranean region- including the Canary Islands-, canary seed is grown today in the cooler regions of the United States and Canada.
- High quality canary seed should be golden yellow (green canary seed is immature), sweet-smelling and glossy.
- The nutritional breakdown of canary seed is: 14% protein, 6% fat, 55% carbohydrates and 2% minerals.

Rape
- Considered the daily bread of the canary, rape seed is high in fat.
- Rape is a small round reddish brown seed which should have a pleasant nutty taste, not a rancid or bitter flavor.
- Rape seed boiled for 10 minutes and then rinsed in cold water can be served as a rearing food.
- Nutritional breakdown: 19% protein, 40% fat, 10% carbohydrates and 4% minerals.

Thistle/Nyger
- Quality thistle should be shiny and black; it is considered a tonic seed.
- Thistle is the seed of a plant closely related to the sunflower.
- Thistle is native to Africa and is grown in India, Burma, Nigeria and Ethiopia and imported into the United States. All thistle sold in the U. S. is heat sterilized under regulation by the U.S. Department of Agriculture. This is apparently due to the thistle's invasive tendencies.
- Nutritional breakdown: 17% protein, 32% fat, 15% carbohydrates and 7% minerals.

Hemp
- Hemp is a largish, grey-brown seed with a greenish tinge.
- All hemp in the United States has been sterilized to prevent the seed from sprouting as hemp is very difficult for non experts to distinguish from marijuana. Hemp and marijuana are very closely related- both are scientifically classified as cannabis sativa-but hemp contains significantly lower quantities of THC, the psychoactive substance which produces the effects associated with marijuana usage. Neither people nor birds are affected by hemp because the concentration of THC is simply too low to produce the effect that marijuana does.
- Whether or not sterilization affects the nutrition of the seed is a matter of some debate, but is considered by many bird breeders to have largely destroyed the nutrient value of

the seed.

- Before hemp was required to be sterilized, it was considered invaluable for promoting fertility (it is rich in vitamin E) among breeding canaries. Since unsterilized hemp is now unavailable, reports of increased fertility problems have risen steadily.
- Anecdotal reports from breeders indicate that the sterilization process is ineffective as approximately 50% of hemp seeds will often sprout.
- The sterilization process makes the hull of the hemp seed extremely hard and nearly impossible for canaries to crack, resulting in a great deal of waste. For this reason, hemp is generally cracked before serving it. The quickest way to crack it is to process for a short time it in an electric coffee grinder.
- Cracked hemp becomes rancid very quickly due to its high oil content so it must be refrigerated or frozen to maintain freshness.
- The seed contains all eight essential amino acids, essential fatty acids (including omega-3 and omega-6).
- Nutritional breakdown: 22% protein, 36% carbohydrates, 30% fat and 4% minerals.

Flaxseed/Linseed

- Seed of the common Flax plant, which has been used as a source of fiber for making linen since ancient times. It is found wild today throughout North America in prairies, open meadows and along roadways.
- Flaxseed has a nutty, buttery flavor when fresh.
- Assists with the molting process in canaries; considered a tonic seed. Very rich in protein and oils, it is fed during the molt to provide plumage with a glossy luster.
- High in antioxidants and soothing to the digestive tract.
- Has been used for treatment of inflammation associated with gout in humans.

Flax: A, seed container; B, branch.

- Contains hormone-balancing lignans and plant phytoestrogens and may improve fertility in hens by stabilizing the estrogen-progesterone ratio and improving the functioning of a hen's reproductive organs. Fertility in males may also be improved as flaxseed seems to play a role in the health of sperm.
- Flaxseed can have a laxative effect, as can all high fat foods.
- Usually included in canary seed mixes in whole seed form, but can also be served ground as flaxseed meal.
- Flaxseed contains the essential fatty acids omega-3, alpha-linolenic acid and linoleic acid. Essential fatty acids are vital to the proper development of organs and the immune system and to overall maintenance of health. Supplementation with essential fatty acids is very important to healthy skin and plumage and can dramatically improve skin and

feather problems.

- Flaxseed is one of the richest plant sources of omega-3 fatty acids.
- Flaxseed can become rancid very quickly, especially after being ground. Store in tightly covered containers in the refrigerator or freezer. Whole seeds will keep for several months refrigerated or indefinitely frozen.
- Stabilized flaxseed is available. This has been treated with zinc and vitamin B_6 to improve taste and prevent rancidity.
- Nutritional breakdown: 21% protein, 34% fat and 24% carbohydrates.

Poppy/Maw

- This is the seed of the opium poppy.
- Bluish colored poppy seed is considered to be superior. It should smell fresh and sweet.
- Poppy has a constipating effect and is used for treatment of loose stools. It is relished by feeding hens.
- Old canary books frequently refer to serving it to sick birds on bread soaked in milk.
- One teaspoon of poppy seed contains 15 calories and 0.5 grams of protein, 1.25 grams of fat and 0.66 grams of carbohydrates. It is a good source of calcium (41 mg) and potassium (20mg).
- Nutritional breakdown: 12% protein, 70% fat and 18% carbohydrates.

Sunflower

- Usually fed to canaries as fine chips. Often recommended for use in conditioning and nestling foods.
- Today sunflower seed is often used in place of hemp to increase fertility levels during the breeding season. Considered by many to be the best whole food source of Vitamin E, although others recommend soaked wheat.
- Care must be taken with feeding sunflower seed outside of the breeding season- or in excessive amounts at any time of the year- as gout can easily result.
- One teaspoon of raw sunflower chips contains 17 calories and 0.68 grams of protein, 1.49 grams of fat and 0.56 grams of carbohydrates. Sunflower is a good source of potassium (21 mg) and is rich in vitamin E.
- Nutritional breakdown: 14% protein, 73% fat and 13% carbohydrates.

Oats

- Easily digested and of assistance in increasing metabolism.
- Used to speed the molt.
- One teaspoon of plain rolled oats contains 3 calories and 0.14 grams of protein, 0.06 grams of fat and 0.54 grams of carbohydrates.

- Nutritional breakdown: 10% protein, 78% carbohydrates, and 12% fat.

Sesame
- A small, cream-colored seed.
- One teaspoon of whole, unhulled sesame seeds contains 17 calories and 0.53 grams of protein, 1.49 grams of fat and 0.7 grams of carbohydrates. It is a good source of calcium (29 mg) and potassium (14 mg).

Anise
- Anise seed smells like licorice and has long been noted for its ability to ease digestive disturbances.
- One teaspoon contains 7 calories and 0.37 grams of protein, 0.33 grams of fat and 1.05 grams of carbohydrates. It is a good source of calcium (14 mg), potassium (30 mg) and vitamin A (7 IU).

Fennel

- Fennel seeds are yellowish-brown and crescent-shaped. A close relative of dill, it has a licorice-like aroma.
- Fennel was used for centuries as both a spice and a food preservative.
- Soothing to the digestive system, it can be used for gastric upsets as it acts as an antispasmodic agent.
- Generally given as a whole seed, but the seeds can also be ground.
- It is a good source of calcium (24 mg), potassium (34 mg) and vitamin A.

Fennel

- One teaspoon contains 7 calories and 0.32 grams of protein, 0.3 grams of fat and 1.05 grams of carbohydrates.

Spray Millet
- A dried, harvested stalk of millet.
- Nutritional breakdown: 15% protein, 6% fats and 51% carbohydrates.

Bee Pollen
- Easily digestible, complete food containing all 22 necessary nutrients. A good conditioning, nestling and molting food.
- Excellent source of protein, amino acids, enzymes and coenzymes, vitamins and minerals. High in calcium and B-complex vitamins.
- Care should be made to ensure that pollen has been bee collected. Some products have actually been harvested by humans from plants.

- Once you have located a source of high quality bee pollen, do not change. Nutritional content varies widely from supplier to supplier.

Spirulina
- Microscopic blue-green algae which is sold as a fine, dark blue-green powder.
- Tastes and smells mild, similar to seaweed but without the salt content.
- Aids in male fertility by supplying the amino acid arginine, which comprises a large proportion of seminal fluid.
- Used during the molt to promote rich feather color.
- Promotes chick growth.
- Highly concentrated and absorbable source of protein; vitamins A, D and K; calcium; selenium; phytonutrients; all eight essential amino acids and ten of the twelve non-essential amino acids.
- Contains B_{12}, which is difficult to obtain from vegetable sources.
- Contains biologically complete proteins, which means that it provides all eight essential amino acids in the proper ratio.
- Spirulina contains amino acids in a form which is five times easier to digest than that found in meat or soy protein.
- Contains natural pigment phytonutrients including phycocyanin, chlorophyll, carotenes and xanthophylls which assist in developing color in feathering.
- Nutritional analysis: 55-70% protein, 6-8% fat, 15-25% carbohydrates and 7-13% minerals.
- Spirulina is safe for daily use, but it can cause diarrhea and digestive upset if fed in excessive quantities. Those who feed it to canaries generally place it in a salt shaker and sprinkle a small quantity over soft food. It can also be mixed into egg food and other soft foods but care should be taken to not use too great a quantity as it will turn the entire mixture green, which seems to be somewhat off-putting for many birds.

Nutritional Yeast Flakes
- Nutritional yeast is grown specifically for its nutritional benefits. The living organism is killed by exposure to high heat.
- High in protein (52%), low in fat, and rich in vitamins and minerals, especially B-complex.
- Yeast flakes are the best source of B vitamins- superior to Brewer's yeast, a byproduct of the brewing industry which has a bitter flavor which is often rejected by birds.
- Nutritional yeast flakes have a nutty-cheesy flavor.
- WARNING: never feed active dry yeast or baker's yeast, as it will rob the body of nutrients. Baked products or pasteurized products containing yeast are fine- the living organisms have been killed.

Wheat Germ, Raw

- Wheat germ is the embryo of the wheat berry. It is a rich source of vitamins, including vitamin E.
- Some breeders use wheat germ oil to push birds into breeding condition quickly, which can lead to higher rates of infertility. Raw wheat germ provides a smaller quantity of vitamin E and additional nutrition and is thought to bring birds into condition more slowly.
- High in carbohydrates- approximately 54% of its calories are derived from carbohydrates.
- Easily becomes rancid so it must be refrigerated or frozen in tightly sealed containers to maintain freshness.
- One teaspoon of raw wheat germ provides 0.5 calories, 0.03 grams of protein, 0.01 grams of fat and 0.08 grams of carbohydrates.

Texturized Vegetable Protein (TVP)

- A dehydrated product made from a process which isolates the proteins from soy flour. Although the product is available flavored, only the unflavored product should be used in feeding canaries. It is important to check labels when buying TVP to ensure that no salt or other additives have been included.
- TVP can be kept in dehydrated state at room temperature for six months if stored in an airtight container.
- One gram of TVP contains 61% protein, 3% fat and 36% carbohydrates.

Nutritional Analysis Quick Comparison Chart

Seed	Protein (grams)/%	Fat (grams)/%	Carbohydrate (grams)/%
Canary	14%	6%	55%
Rape	19%	40%	10%
Bee Pollen	35%	2%	55%
Thistle/Nyger	17%	32%	15%
Hemp	22%	36%	30%
Flax/Linseed	21%	34%	24%
Poppy/Maw	0.5 / 12%	1.25 / 70%	0.66 / 18%
Sunflower	0.68 / 14%	1.49 / 73%	0.56 / 13%
Oats	0.14 / 10%	0.06 / 12%	0.54 / 78%
Sesame	0.53 / 11%	1.49 / 73%	0.7 / 16%
Anise	0.37 / 18%	0.33 / 39%	1.05 / 43%
Fennel	0.32 / 15%	0.3 / 36%	1.05 / 49%
Millet, Spray	15%	6%	51%
Wheat Germ, Raw	23%	23%	54%
Texturized Vegetable Protein (TVP)	61%	3%	36%
Spirulina	55-70%	6-8%	15-25%

Where grams are noted, all amounts are as measured in one teaspoon.

Nutritional data for foods also consumed by humans (poppy, sunflower, oats, sesame, anise, fennel, and wheat germ) from information provided by the USDA.

Fruits and Vegetables

Canaries can be fed a wide variety of fruits and vegetables. Birds should be gradually accustomed to eating fresh foods as canaries that are unused to eating them can develop diarrhea and other digestive upsets. Fruits and vegetables should always be washed thoroughly before cutting or serving regardless of their source. I soak all vegetables in cold water to which apple cider vinegar has been added for a short period before serving.

Fruits

Apple
- 84% water content makes them a good food to feed during the molt.
- High in fiber, prevents constipation.
- Apples contain malic acid and tartaric acids, which prevent fermentation in the intestines, and pectin, a soluble fiber which encourages the growth of beneficial bacteria in the digestive tract.
- Apples also contain flavonoids, which are thought to improve immune system functioning.
- Apple seeds should not be fed to birds.
- Apples are included on the list of foods on which pesticide residues are most frequently found. For this reason, apples to be fed to birds should be organically grown.

Banana
- In researching banana, I discovered that it is noted frequently as a rich source of potassium, but there are other sources which provide more in a smaller serving (for instance- cantaloupe, broccoli, sunflower seeds and others). Possibly considered high in potassium due to the amount contained in a single serving- which is an <u>entire</u> banana. Most canaries cannot and should not eat an entire banana!
- Bananas are actually richer in vitamin B_6 than in potassium.
- High in carbohydrates and a good source of natural fiber.
- Soothing food for digestive upsets; unusual in that they assist in treating both diarrhea and constipation.

Melon- Cantaloupe and Honeydew
- Cantaloupe is an excellent source of vitamins A and C.
- Honeydew is a good source of vitamin C.
- Both melons are more than 90% water, which makes them cooling foods to serve during the summer and the molt.

- Canaries love cantaloupe sliced or cubed.

Orange
- Loved by canaries- simply slice into quarters.
- Excellent source of vitamin C and a good source of vitamin A and calcium.

Raspberry
- Excellent source of vitamin C.
- Does contain oxalates and should not be fed to canaries during the breeding season as oxalates bind calcium.
- Contains a natural painkiller.

Strawberry
- Strawberries have one of the highest levels of pesticide contaminates. For this reason, be careful to serve only organically grown strawberries to birds.
- Very high in vitamin C, K and the B vitamin folate. Contains Omega-3 fatty acids.

<u>Vegetables</u>

Broccoli- Flowers and Leaves
- Considered an excellent source of vitamins A and C and a very good source of B vitamins, protein, omega 3 fatty acids and calcium. Also contains vitamin E.
- Leaves are much higher in vitamin A than are the flowers.
- High in fiber and in minerals.
- Can be served whole or chopped fine.

Broccoli Rabe
- Pronounced broccoli rob, it is also known as rapini, rabe, choy sum and Chinese flowering cabbage.
- Broccoli rabe flowers appear similar to the broccoli's florets. Despite the similarity in appearance broccoli rabe is not a type of broccoli, but they do belong to the same plant family.
- Slightly bitter taste, strong flavor.
- Rich in beta carotene and vitamin C.

Carrot
- The best source of natural vitamin A, an excellent source of vitamin K, and a good source of vitamin C.
- Adds brightness to the color of the plumage when fed during the molt.

- Chopped fine, it can be mixed with eggfood or other soft food.
- Cooked carrots are an excellent food for weaning baby canaries.
- Carrot greens are also nutritious and are readily accepted by canaries.

Corn
- Can be fed on the cob- birds will even learn to turn the cobs over to get at the kernels on the bottom, which considering that the cobs can weigh more than a canary is no small feat.
- Some breeders mix frozen corn in with their eggfood, but there is a lot of waste as birds toss the kernels around the cage without eating them.
- High in carbohydrates- birds love it, but it should be fed sparingly. It has been equated to candy for canaries!

Cucumbers
- Excellent molting and summer food due to its high water content.
- Simply slice the cucumber lengthwise down the middle and serve. Birds will hollow out the skin.
- The cucumber's nutrition is primarily in its peel, which has vitamin A and fiber. Overall, however, the cucumber is very low in nutrients.

Dandelion Greens
- One of the most nutritious and least expensive vegetables available.
- Dandelion greens are an excellent source of vitamin A, C, K, D and B complex; they contain 20% protein- twice that of spinach; and are a good source of minerals, including trace minerals.
- Care must be taken to gather dandelion greens from areas that have not been treated with chemicals of any kind- including chemical fertilizers, herbicides and pesticides. Washing will not remove these contaminants.

Endive
- Reportedly first produced in 1850 when a Belgium farmer discovered that some chicory roots stored in his cellar had sprouted and produced an edible vegetable.
- Endive is actually the second growth of the chicory plant- the first growth is chopped off, the roots are dug up and then brought indoors where a second growth is artificially forced.
- Endive is grown indoors in a dark, cool environment. Because of this it does not require treatment for pesticides, which makes it great for birds!
- It has a slightly bitter taste.
- There are no nutritional differences between red and white endive.

- Higher in potassium than banana with fewer carbohydrates.
- Very high in minerals such as calcium, iron and selenium.
- Excellent source of vitamins A, C, K and folate. Contains vitamin E and B vitamins.

Kale
- Contains more vitamin A than spinach and twice as much lutein, an antioxidant.
- Excellent source of vitamins A and C and a good source of calcium.

Lettuce- Iceberg
- This is a nutritionally empty food, containing little more than fiber and water.
- Feeding it causes diarrhea; it is not a good food for canaries.

Lettuce- Romaine
- Good source of vitamins A and C. Also a good source of several B vitamins.
- Contains calcium, omega-3 fatty acids and protein.

Pumpkin
- Raw pumpkin is an excellent source of vitamin A. Simply cut into chunks and serve.

Spinach
- Serve sparingly due to its high levels of oxalic acid.
- Excellent source of vitamin A and lutein.

Sweet Potato
- Excellent source of vitamin A and a good source of vitamin C.
- Can be served raw and grated into soft food.
- Canned sweet potatoes can also be served- drain and cook until tender, then mash.

Fruits and Vegetables for Canaries:
Vitamin and Mineral Chart

Items are listed as poor (providing little or none), fair (providing a small portion), good and excellent sources of the listed nutrient. It is obviously more economical to serve small portions of foods which are excellent sources of nutrition than large portions of those things which provide little nutrition. All fruits and vegetables are served raw.

Fruit or Vegetable	Vitamin A	B Vitamins	Vitamin C	Vitamin E	Calcium	Other Minerals
Apple	Poor	Poor	Fair	Poor	Poor	Poor
Banana	Poor	Fair	Fair	Poor	Poor	Fair
Bell Pepper	Poor	Poor	Excellent	Poor	Poor	Poor
Broccoli- Flowers	Good	Good	Excellent	Poor	Fair	Good
Broccoli- Leaves	Excellent	Good	Excellent	Poor	Fair	Good
Broccoli Rabe	Excellent	Good	Excellent	Fair	Fair	Fair
Carrot	Excellent	Fair	Fair	Poor	Poor	Fair
Corn, Sweet	Poor	Fair	Fair	Poor	Poor	Fair
Cucumber	Poor	Poor	Fair	Poor	Poor	Poor
Dandelion Greens	Excellent	Good	Excellent	Fair	Excellent	Good
Endive	Excellent	Fair	Fair	Poor	Fair	Fair
Grapefruit	Fair	Poor	Excellent	Poor	Poor	Poor
Kale	Excellent	Fair	Excellent	Poor	Fair	Good
Lamb's Quarters	Excellent	Fair	Excellent	Poor	Excellent	Excellent
Lettuce- Iceberg	Poor	Poor	Poor	Poor	Poor	Poor
Lettuce- Romaine	Good	Fair	Good	Poor	Fair	Fair
Melon- Cantaloupe	Good	Poor	Excellent	Poor	Poor	Poor
Melon- Honeydew	Poor	Poor	Good	Poor	Poor	Poor

Fruit or Vegetable	Vitamin A	B Vitamins	Vitamin C	Vitamin E	Calcium	Other Minerals
Nectarine	Fair	Poor	Fair	Poor	Poor	Poor
Orange	Fair	Poor	Excellent	Poor	Fair	Poor
Peach	Fair	Poor	Fair	Poor	Poor	Poor
Pear	Poor	Poor	Fair	Poor	Poor	Poor
Plum	Fair	Poor	Fair	Poor	Poor	Poor
Pumpkin	Excellent	Poor	Fair	Poor	Poor	Fair
Raspberry	Poor	Poor	Excellent	Poor	Poor	Fair
Strawberries	Poor	Poor	Excellent	Poor	Poor	Poor
Spinach	Excellent	Fair	Excellent	Fair	Fair	Good
Sweet Potato	Excellent	Fair	Fair	Poor	Fair	Fair
Tangerine	Good	Poor	Good	Poor	Poor	Poor

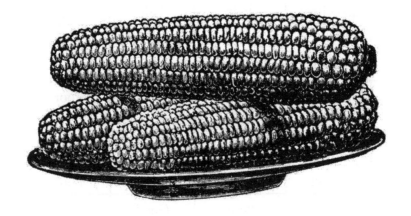

Herbs, Natural Supplements and Their Uses

Very little study has been done on the use of herbs in small birds and little information exists to guide one in their uses. While I have personally used all of the herbs discussed in this chapter, dosing is largely a matter of trial and error due to the inconsistent quality of supplements. I prefer to err on the side of caution and use less rather than more of an herb when first giving it to canaries. Carefully monitor the bird's response- when an amount seems to be therapeutic, remain at that dosage level. More is not always better, but in fact can be dangerous! Moderation should always be the rule when using these substances.

This listing is by no means complete. A wide range of herbs and other supplements exist, each with their own reputed benefits. I have sought to include here the more common and widely available. No attempt has been made to list every possible use of each substance but only those which are relevant to the problems and conditions breeders of canaries commonly encounter.

While many herbs and supplements may be provided in whole form, teas are often the preferred form of administration. Birds will often initially reject herbal teas supplied as drinking water. If this is the case, drops of tea may be administered by placing them in the beak using a clean, sterile eyedropper.

IMPORTANT DISCLAIMER: I am not a holistic veterinarian or a trained herbalist and do not provide the following information as a recommendation for medical treatment but only to present an educational overview of the most commonly used herbs, spices and nutritional substances. Always consult a professional before administering any medical treatment yourself. While serious side effects are less common than with pharmaceutical compounds, they can occur.

Alfalfa

- Alfalfa is a member of the legume family and is closely related to beans and peas.
- Leaves of the alfalfa plant are very nutritious and contain vitamins and minerals including E and K, calcium, magnesium and potassium. Alfalfa is an excellent source of chlorophyll and carotene. It also provides amino acids.
- Alfalfa seeds should not be fed as they contain the slightly toxic amino acid L-cavanine. Sprouted alfalfa seeds are safe.
- It is thought to possess detoxifying and antifungal properties.
- Alfalfa can be purchased as small bales in most pet food stores,

Alfalfa

where it is marketed for rabbits and similar small animals. It should be finely chopped or broken up and served on an occasional basis. Larger pieces are simply played with and encourage the thoughts of canary hens to turn toward nesting rather more than a breeder might care for- resulting in nests built of alfalfa in the flight cage!

Aloe Vera

- Aloe vera is a succulent plant belonging to the lily family which is native to Madagascar and portions of Africa. It has been commonly grown as a houseplant for many years.
- Aloe has been used for centuries as a topical treatment for burns, bites, cuts, abrasions, rashes and other wounds and skin irritations. Aloe acts as a natural antibiotic and assists in prevention of infection when used on injured skin. It also provides pain relief, reduces inflammation and itching and speeds healing.
- Traditionally, a piece of fresh leaf is broken from the plant and the clear gel is squeezed or scraped from the fleshy inner part of the leaf. Commercial liquid, cream and gel products are now readily available. In general, liquid aloe is used internally and for mixing with water for misting; gel products are used topically.
- When purchasing commercial products, look for those which are pure (more than 98%) and avoid extracts and reconstituted products. Aloe should always be the first product on the list of ingredients.
- Liquid aloe vera concentrate relieves a number of digestive complaints when taken internally and can be used for misting when diluted in water.
- Aloe juice concentrate is also used internally for detoxification. Reports of the recovery of extremely ill parrots treated internally with aloe concentrate abound, although use in canaries has not been documented. Care should be taken with internal use of aloe juice as overuse can lead to potassium depletion.
- A powerful laxative can be made from aloe latex, a substance taken from specialized cells located along the inner leaf skin. This extract is usually removed and dried into a yellow powder. Improperly processed aloe vera juice can contain the laxative compound found in aloe latex and cause cramping, diarrhea or loose stools. Should these symptoms occur, discard the product and replace it.
- As common sense dictates, all wounds and injuries should be cleaned thoroughly before applying aloe. Liberal application of cream or gel can be made as needed for burns, two to three times daily for cuts and superficial wounds and four times daily for relief from insect bites and other skin irritations.
- Aloe vera juice must be refrigerated to maintain freshness.

Calendula Petals

- Also known as pot marigold. This plant should not be confused with more common garden marigolds of the tagetes family, which have a pungent odor.

- Originally native to Europe and Africa, calendula has been used by Europeans as food and medicinally since the 12th century. It is now common in herb gardens worldwide.
- Calendula flowers are yellow, orange, or red-orange and are often referred to as "Poor Man's Saffron."
- Calendula has been shown in studies to have astringent, antibacterial, antifungal and anti-inflammatory properties. It may also boost the immune system.
- Dried petals are readily available from most bulk herb sources.
- Calendula petals provide a richness of color to the feathers when fed during the molt.
- Cooled calendula tea can provide some relief to burns, wounds, sprains and skin irritations and also can be used as an eyewash for eye infections.
- Calendula can be used topically three to four times per day.
- To make calendula tea, pour one cup of boiling water over ½ teaspoon of flower tops or petals and steep for 10 minutes. Strain through a coffee filter and cool.

Chamomile, German

- German chamomile is preferred to Roman chamomile as it has more potent medicinal properties.
- Native of Europe and western Asia, chamomile flowers have been used medicinally by herbalists for thousands of years. Dried flowers are readily available from bulk herb suppliers.
- Chamomile is used primarily as a tea to treat digestive disturbances, as a mild sedative and to treat skin irritation.
- Some suggestion is that it may have a tonic effect on muscles of the reproductive system, therefore making it useful for treating egg binding in hens.
- Chamomile tea is excellent for providing as a sole source of drinking water to sick birds in hospital cages as it soothes the stomach and keeps birds calm. It is usually readily accepted as it has a pleasant taste.
- Chamomile has been used as a worming agent for some time. It is gentler than other faster acting herbal wormers and has anti-inflammatory effects which can help relieve the effects of parasites on the lining of the intestinal muscosa.
- Chamomile tea can be boiled and the steam used for treatment of respiratory problems. (Of course, care must always be taken to ensure that the bird is not burned by hot steam!)

Chickweed

- A common weed in the United States, it usually grows in low-growing mats or entangled in other plants.

- Chickweed can be differentiated from other plants of similar appearance by the following characteristic: a line of tiny hairs runs up only one side of the stem, switching sides at each pair of leaves.
- Care must be taken to ensure that only herbicide-free chickweed is used. Washing will not remove herbicides!
- This plant has been used by canary breeders for a very long time as a green food. Many old breeding books state that it is an excellent breeding conditioner.
- Chickweed is highly nutritious, containing vitamins B_6, B_{12} and C.
- It may be of use in treating gout.
- Known to soothe and mildly lubricate the upper digestive system, but large quantities can have a laxative effect.

Dandelion

- Originally native to Europe and Asia, dandelion was brought to the United States by the early colonists to provide a source of greens early in the spring and has spread everywhere since then.
- In some places, it is called wild endive.
- Although in Europe this plant is highly valued and grown commercially, in the United States dandelion is generally wild-gathered and special care must be taken to gather only herbicide- and pesticide-free plants. Also, dandelions growing in chemically fertilized lawns absorb these chemicals and should not be used.
- Dandelion greens are an excellent source of early spring greens for canaries as they are highly nutritious and a good breeding conditioner.
- Dandelion greens are an excellent source of vitamin A, C, K, D and B complex; they contain 20% protein-twice that of spinach; and are a good source of minerals, including trace minerals.

Dandelion

- The greens stimulate the appetite and can improve digestion and the absorption of nutrients. Considered a tonic and valued for its detoxifying properties.
- Dried dandelion flowers can be used as a pain killer as they possess mild analgesic properties.

Dill

- Originally native to southeast Europe and Asia, it is now a common garden plant worldwide.
- Related to fennel, it has a distinctive aroma.
- Dill was used to preserve food before refrigeration.
- Studies have shown dill tea to be an effective and gentle treatment for digestive problems. Soothing to the digestive system, it acts as an antispasmodic agent.
- Dill has also been shown to inhibit the growth of several bacteria which cause infectious diarrhea.
- Some studies have also shown that dill may provide some assistance in discouraging parasites.
- Tea can be prepared by using two teaspoons of seed to each cup of boiling water.
- Usually served as a whole seed in a seed mix, but it can also be ground and added to soft food.

Kelp

- Kelp is brown algae which grow only in the sea. The term kelp can apply to any of a number of different seaweeds that belong to the order *Laminariales* or *Fucales*. In the United States, rockweed is the type most commonly cultivated for dietary supplements.
- Kelp provides protein and carotenoids as well as vitamins and minerals. It also supplies iodine.
- Kelp possesses antibacterial, antifungal and antiviral properties. Additionally, it stimulates the immune system.
- Used often by breeders of colorbred birds, especially bronze canaries. Kelp is thought to help develop the dark coloration in the legs which is sought after in bronze birds.

Mint

- A wide variety of mints exist, some of which are of more use than others. Mints suitable for consumption by canaries include peppermint, spearmint and apple mint.
- The most commonly used mint for relief of digestive complaints is peppermint, which has long been used to promote digestion. It also has a sedative effect.
- Peppermint essential oil has some of the strongest antibiotic properties tested in herbal preparations. It has also shown some antiviral effects.
- Spearmint has benefits similar to that of peppermint and is a commonly grown garden plant. Fresh leaves can easily be added to the diet of canaries by simply mixing them in with other green food provided. A single leaf would be ample for one canary.
- PENNYROYAL should never be fed as it is toxic.

Plantain

- Common weed widespread throughout North America.
- As with all wild-harvested plants, care should be taken to gather only those which are herbicide and pesticide free.
- Nutritionally, plantain is very high in vitamins A, C and K.
- It possesses anti-inflammatory and antibacterial properties which make it useful for a variety of digestive and respiratory ailments.
- Plantain can assist in relieving intestinal inflammation and diarrhea.
- Plantain stimulates the appetite.
- Best used fresh, both leaves and seed heads are relished by canaries.

Raspberry

- The dried leaves and fresh fruit of both red and black raspberries are medicinally useful.
- WARNING: raspberry leaves should only be used when completely dry- wilted leaves can cause nausea due to the presence of toxins that are present during the drying process.
- The fruit is an excellent source of vitamin C.
- Raspberry leaves are useful for digestive complaints and can resolve mild diarrhea.
- The dried powdered leaf can be mixed into soft food.
- Excellent tonic for hens- traditionally used to improve the tone and elasticity of muscles around the reproductive organs. However, excessive amounts can cause uterine contractions in mammals, so the use of raspberry during breeding season is not advisable.
- Cooled raspberry leaf tea can be used as an eyewash for relief of symptoms of eye infections. Steep one teaspoon of dried leaf to eight ounces of hot water for several minutes and then cool. Strain through a coffee filter and then combine with sufficient sterile saline solution (available wherever contact lens supplies are sold) to produce a slightly colored solution.
- Full strength, cooled raspberry leaf tea can also be used to relieve minor skin irritations.

Red Clover

- A member of the pea family originally introduced from Europe to the United States as a feed crop for livestock, it has naturalized throughout North America. Clover is recognizable by its three-lobed leaves. Red clover is distinguished from other clovers by its red globe-shaped flowers, its soft, hairy stems and the presence of a small carrot-like taproot.
- The dried flower head is the medicinally useful part of the plant.
- Red clover is very nutritious- it contains protein; vitamins A, B-complex and C; and the minerals calcium, magnesium and potassium.
- It possesses antibiotic, analgesic and anti-inflammatory properties and is noted for its blood-purifying, tonic properties.
- Red clover is useful for treating skin disorders and for speeding recovery from viral respiratory infections.
- Cooled tea can be applied for symptomatic relief of dry, itchy skin.
- Dried red clover can be added to soft food or mixed in the daily seed mix. Canaries seem to enjoy the flavor and will often pick it out and eat it first.
- Red clover does have blood thinning properties due to the presence of the compound coumarin. For this reason, it should not be given to birds with internal or external bleeding.
- Excessive consumption of red clover has been shown to be toxic in livestock- as with all herbs and supplements, moderation is the key to safe use.
- Red clover should not be given during the breeding season to birds you wish to breed.

Witch Hazel

- A small, common shrub native to the Eastern United States, the first settlers were introduced to its medicinal uses by Native Americans.
- At one time considered to be a household necessity due to its usefulness, witch hazel is generally applied topically to relieve skin inflammation, burns, bruises, itching from insect bites and to promote the healing of skin infections.
- Distilled extract of witch hazel is preserved with alcohol and thus care should be taken when using it near the head of a small bird. It should not be given internally.
- Witch hazel is generally inferior to aloe vera for treatment of skin problems.

Yarrow

- Native to Asia, yarrow now grows wild throughout the northern hemisphere. It is characterized by flat-topped clusters of small flowers and its featherlike leaves. Highly aromatic, with a pungency similar to that of mothballs.

- Achillea, its genus name, is derived from the mythical Greek character Achilles, who carried it with his army to treat battle wounds. Yarrow has also been called staunchweed and soldier's woundwort.

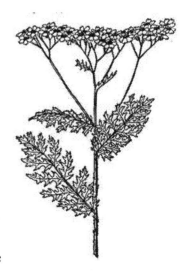

- The leaves were eaten as a popular vegetable through the 17th century.

- Yarrow has astringent, tonic, anti-inflammatory and antimicrobial properties. It is used topically to treat wounds, cuts and abrasions. Yarrow stops bleeding and disinfects wounds. It has also been used to expel worms, although its effectiveness as a wormer is marginal.

- To treat wounds and stop bleeding, crush the herb as finely as possible and apply directly to the wound. A very effective natural powder for stopping bleeding can be made from a 50/50 mix of dried yarrow and cayenne.

- Cooled tea can be used to relieve pain and itching of the skin.

- Dried yarrow is noted for repelling fleas, mosquitoes and biting flies.

- Yarrow has been shown in studies to inhibit the growth of a number of feather-degrading bacteria. Recent studies at Ohio Wesleyan University have shown that wild birds select nesting materials with antimicrobial agents such as yarrow to line their nests.

- It is useful for treating respiratory ailments as it has antibacterial and expectorant properties as well as helping to improve respiratory blood vessel circulation.

- Yarrow has been used for treating intestinal inflammations, bleeding and infections.

- This herb is very bitter and not readily taken by birds so administration via drops of tea into the beak is preferred. Allergic skin reactions to this plant are fairly common.

- Yarrow can be toxic in large quantities, especially when consumed over an extended period. Moderation is key to safe use. Do not use this herb on birds during the breeding season- in humans, it has been used as a contraceptive and may have similar effects on birds.

Bee Pollen and Canaries

As canary breeders, the use of nutritional supplements can be confusing. Frequently one must rely on the advice of fellow breeders who may not know the exact properties of a given substance or its proper administration. Lack of good information can lead to poor results; many breeders may assume a supplement to be ineffective when in fact the supplement has not been given a fair trial due to a variety of factors including poor quality and improper administration.

One supplement I have found to be particularly useful in my birdroom is bee pollen. Bee pollen is poorly understood and poorly utilized by many canary fanciers due in part to insufficient factual data regarding this supplement. The variety of ways in which this is utilized also tends to provide evidence for the theory that the typical breeder using it is not quite sure how to do so most effectively.

In its most natural form, bee pollen is a fine powder composed of microscopic particles of the male reproductive organ of the flower called the stamen. This powder collects on the legs of bees as they journey from flower to flower gathering nectar. Pollen is harvested when the bees return to their hives- each bee passes through a pollen screen consisting of a metal grid which scrapes approximately 60% of the pollen off while leaving sufficient quantity for the bee colony to support itself. The pollen then falls below into a pollen drawer which can be removed and emptied by the beekeeper.

Bee pollen supplies proteins, carbohydrates, fats, enzymes and coenzymes, carotenes, vitamins and minerals necessary for normal growth and development. It also contains HGH, hormones and natural antibiotics. Studies on generations of mice fed exclusively on bee pollen have shown no signs of malnourishment and bee pollen is often referred to as a "complete food." It is approximately 35% protein, 55% carbohydrates, 2% fatty acids and 3% vitamins and minerals.

The nutritional value of bee pollen varies widely depending on what the colony has fed on- buckwheat, citrus, and sunflower being poor sources of nutrition and clovers being better sources of quality pollen. Crude protein levels can be as low as 9% and as high as 37% depending on the colony's food sources. Containing the amino acids aspartic acid, serine, glutamic acid, proline, glycine, alanine, leucine, tyrosine, cystine, threonine, valine, methionine, isoleucine, phenylalanine, histidine, lysine, arginine and tryptophan, bee pollen is an excellent source of vital amino acids. Fat levels can vary from as little as less than 1% to almost 3%, but the average is about 2%. (Information from "Nutritional Value of Bee Collected Pollens, A Report for the Rural Industries Research and Development Corporation" by D. C. Somerville, published May 2001.) Pollen contains high concentrations of B vitamins as well as vitamin A, C, D and E and also the minerals calcium, manganese, phosphorous, iron, sulphur, silicon, sodium, potassium, aluminum, magnesium, copper and others. It also contains natural pigments such as flavoxanthine, xanthophyll epoxide, carotene, epiphasic carotenoids, falvonols, ethylic ether, quercitin, zeaxanthine, lycopene, crocetin and others.

Improperly stored and handled bee pollen loses 76% of its potency within twelve months, thus pollen should be frozen to preserve nutritive value. Low moisture, granulated pollen is also preferable in that it maintains freshness longer. The best storage method is to freeze the pollen and keep at room temperature only the quantity which will be used within a few days.

Breeders vary greatly in how they use bee pollen- some pass it out as though it were gold, only allowing a certain number of granules per bird while others offer it free choice in a finger drawer. I prefer to sprinkle a liberal amount on top of the dry nestling food offered in the breeding cages at all times. During other times of the year it is offered sprinkled on top of soft food or dry conditioning food. Mixing bee pollen with other foods increases the likelihood that the birds will fail to eat it.

My birds usually eat the pollen before anything else and feed it well to their chicks. Babies fed bee pollen gain size faster and have excellent feather quality, good resistance to illness and mature quickly. Weaning chicks seem to enjoy pollen and can eat it before they are able to crack seeds. My birds have access to pollen at all times during the molt and are offered pollen a few times a week during conditioning for breeding. Birds fed pollen throughout the year are often the first to come into full breeding condition and display excellent fertility levels.

The cost of bee pollen is not prohibitive given the quality of results seen from its use. Savvy shoppers can locate high quality bee pollen for less than $5 a pound and considering the amount necessary a pound of pollen lasts a considerable length of time. With a population of a hundred or so birds and a liberal feeding of the supplement, I use between fifteen and twenty pounds a year in my aviary.

The Soy Controversy

In the past few years, there has developed a controversy about feeding soy products to birds. Some of the effects reportedly caused by feeding soy to birds include beak and bone deformities, goiter, immune system disorders, infertility, premature maturation, and aggression.

Every one of these issues could be caused by myriad things and no scientific research has been done on the subject to either prove or disprove these claims. It is interesting to note that these claims do not come from actual breeders for the most part but from anti soy groups.

Although a considerable number of different articles state these claims, each one refers back to the information provided by the same anti soy group- which is based on the report of a <u>single</u> report from a married couple, Richard and Valerie James, who breed birds in New Zealand. The James' reportedly switched to a new type of bird food which contained soy- the product is never named- and claim that the birds became sick, infertile and developed their adult coloring at an unusually young age. The couple claims that by eliminating the soy-containing food from their flock's diet, the birds were all restored to complete health. The articles state that "many of New Zealand's leading parrot breeders" reported this problem, but Richard and Valerie James are the only ones willing to go public.

Soy- in a variety of forms- is a common ingredient in commercial pet bird foods. Major brands such as ABBA, Scenic, Scott, Harrison, Zupreem, Quiko and Pretty Bird include soy products such at soybean flour and meal, soya oil, etc. in their foods. Orlux eggfood contains "vegetable proteins" which are probably soy-derived and I suspect that CeDe universal rearing food contains soy disguised under the label of "vegetable protein extracts." These are all highly respected companies whose products have been used and valued for some time. One would think that if the dire results of feeding soy reported by the James' were true that problems would be both widespread and obvious. I have personally been feeding soy for years to my birds in the form of TVP and soy protein isolate as two ingredients among many in my nestling and molting foods and have yet to see any ill effects at all.

The single issue about soy which may have merit is premature maturation. For the past two years my birds have come into full song at an unusually early age. I thought this situation rather odd since every breeder I have spoken with tells me that young birds cannot be in full song so young, but I was presented with a birdroom filled with birds that apparently were not aware that they were too young to be mature! Soy opponents would claim that this is caused by soy, but I do not believe it to be the sole cause. A similar phenomenon is occurring in human children in the United States- they are becoming physically mature at earlier and earlier ages due in large part to vastly improved nutritional levels.

Excellent nutrition is likely to be the source of the early maturation I am witnessing in my birdroom as well. My birds are the recipients of a very whole-food centered diet program which utilizes a wide range of natural foods. I am sure that my holistic, whole-food centered feeding program seems like a great deal of nonsense to the majority of breeders who rely on a spare, basic program or on commercial preparations. They all agree, however, that my birds are exceptionally healthy and vigorous looking. The birds are extremely fertile and with few exceptions are good parents and amiable companions in the aviary. I have never seen a beak or bone deformity, a goiter, an immune system disorder or premature aging in my birdroom and my birds really do eat a great deal of soy.

Anti soy groups state that feeding soy products drastically shorten the life spans of birds. This is somewhat difficult to accept as soy products have been a staple part of the diet in Japan for centuries and the Japanese have the longest average human lifespan in the world. Japanese men and women live an average of six years longer than those in the United States. Apparently the Japanese could live even longer if they only eliminated soy from their diets?

In my experience, soy products are safe to feed canaries. Despite the warnings from those who fear soy in all its forms, I would not be concerned about feeding soy as long as the common sense rule of moderation is followed.

Soy-bean. — *a*, leaf, and spray with pods; *b*, beans.

For Your Information: The Many Names of Soy . . .

Soy is called many things and is sold in many forms.
Some of the names under which soy can be found: soybean meal, soy flour, soya or soja, soy or soybean oil, tofu, texturized vegetable protein (TVP), hydrolyzed vegetable protein, tofu, isolated soy protein, vegetable protein, soy concentrate, Dan dou chi.

To Feed Egg Or Not to Feed Egg, That Is The Question . . .

Eggs have been used by canary breeders for a very long time. Some breeders swear by them, some swear by their egg free diet alternative- in the end what really matters is how are YOUR birds doing?

I am a voracious reader of all things canary related and I am also notorious for picking the brain of any and every breeder I meet. Feeding methods are very different from breeder to breeder- the one truth I have uncovered is that once you have developed a method that works for you, don't change it!

I know breeders who have bred canaries successfully for more than forty years on two servings a day of a nestling food that consists of Petamine nestling food (this used to be called Peep nestling) and mashed, whole boiled egg mixed together. In addition to 80/20 canary seed/rape seed and occasional song food, that's all the birds ever eat- no greens, no fruit, nothing- and the birds are very fertile and very healthy. I've seen others (including my own) who eat better than their owners and are also very fertile and very healthy.

Certain lines of birds (and even individual birds within a line) are more susceptible to developing problems from eating egg than others. (Just as in an entire flight of a hundred birds all fed exactly the same diet there will be skinny and obese birds- some birds are just genetically predisposed to getting fat.) If your line of birds is one which is sensitive to gout or something along that line, don't feed too much egg (yolks or whites) at any time of the year. I have never personally seen a feeding hen develop gout while feeding chicks- even when fed egg yolk every day- but some breeders have reported it happening. My babies get mashed boiled egg yolk during the weaning period as they need the fat and protein and the bright yellow color is attractive to them. After several years of this, I have yet to see any impact on their health. After weaning, birds only receive egg when breeding and occasionally during the molt.

Whatever works for your birds is just fine. Sometimes I think a breeder will run into trouble (which is only to be expected eventually) and pounces on the diet because it's easily manipulated and there is a wealth of conflicting information about the subject. Even experienced breeders who I respect greatly completely disagree on greens. Some believe you should feed lots of them, some believe they should be offered more sparingly. What's a novice breeder to do?

Try to locate a local canary club- there are many which will happily provide assistance to novices. Some, like the Michigan-based DRAGON- Chapter 22 of the American Singer Club- have extensive libraries of canary related articles and members who are happy to mentor new members. Contact the breeder you purchased your birds from and follow his or her method until you know your birds and gain experience, then watch your birds and let THEM dictate what you do! Remember that there is no substitute for diligent husbandry.

If a bird has a problem with the diet you provide your flock, separate him and feed him differently- my fat birds are separated into diet cages frequently (although since I have become more familiar with some of the genetic traits of certain lines I have managed to eliminate part of this tendency toward obesity through selective breeding) and the one bird I have had who had a problem with gout lived separately from the rest- feeding anything beyond plain canary and rape seed led to gout flare-ups until he went to a pet home (with strict dietary instructions). Since there is a genetic component to the tendency to develop gout, eliminating gouty birds from one's breeding program is desirable.

Soft Foods: Nestling Food, Egg Food, Rearing Food

Canaries require soft food of some type to rear their young successfully. While it is true that young will survive and grow on nothing but seed, egg, and greens they will certainly do better if more care is given to their nutritional needs.

If there is an issue about which breeders disagree the most, it is probably the subject of nestling food. Every breeder I have ever encountered has his own special formula which he swears to be the best and it is true, that recipe is the best- *for his birds*.

The novice is best advised to acquire the recipe that the breeder from whom his original stock is purchased uses. The birds are accustomed to this and will accept it readily. Once the novice breeder has become familiar with the birds- and the birds to the breeder- changes can be made to the diet by gradually introducing small amounts of new foods.

Once a food (or feeding system) has been found which works for one's particular birds it is best to stick with it. One of the first things breeders do when they experience problems is change the diet- even when that diet had always been fine before. Resist the temptation to make changes simply for change's sake and do not make radical changes in the midst of breeding season. My birds are accustomed to being presented with all sorts of foods and are open to trying almost anything while birds that have never seen an ear of corn or a slice of orange may be terrified by it. A hen who stays away from the feeding dish because she is uncertain of the strange item it contains is not feeding her chicks, obviously!

Prepared eggfood does not need to be made fresh every day, it can be frozen. Freeze in portions sufficient to last one day, then either thaw overnight in the refrigerator or microwave for twenty to thirty seconds just until thawed enough for the mixture to fall apart and crumble when pushed with a spoon (do not heat until warm). Prepare frozen eggfood as you would normally by mixing with shredded carrots, etc. Some breeders serve frozen eggfood during the summer molt as it stays fresh a little longer. Freezing does change the texture of the boiled egg, but the birds do not seem to care.

A food processor is an essential tool- one can throw shredded wheat, bread or whatever needs to be mixed into it and be finished in very little time. Chopping up eggs in a food processor requires some skill- process eggs for too long and they form a solid mass of egg matter which requires a considerable amount of dry mix to sort out. I have found it best to add the dry ingredients to the food processor and the hard-boiled eggs (with shells intact) together, and then process minimally- just until moist and crumbly.

Traditional Nestling Food

Boil two large eggs for twenty minutes. Cool the eggs, peel the shells and mash them with a fork. Mix sufficient fresh, soft breadcrumbs to make a moist, crumbly texture and sprinkle servings with poppy seed. This mixture is not nutritionally complete, but many thousands of birds were raised successfully on it "back in the old days."

Commercial Nestling Foods

Commercial nestling foods provide breeding birds with nutritious food and save the busy breeder time, but they can be expensive and are sometimes rejected by birds. Many breeders mix the commercial preparations with boiled egg, soak seed or grated carrots to make them more palatable and nutritionally complete.

Care must be taken with some of these foods as they are made from bakery products which contain a great deal of sugar, something chicks are not able to process well for the first three days of life. Most birds love Cédé (pronounced "cee dee") brand eggfood, but it is very sweet- containing about 50% starches and sugars- so it should not be fed for the first few days after hatching.

A large number of different brands are available and each has its own fan base. I have used nearly every brand at one time or another and personally prefer Petamine Nestling from Scott's Feeds because it's one of the least expensive available and it seems to be accepted by most birds. I use it occasionally as an alternative to my own homemade eggfood to provide the birds something different once in a while.

Old Fashioned Nestling Food

This is an old recipe that has been used for years.

1 cup	Dry Bread Crumbs
1 cup	High Protein Mixed Baby Cereal
1 cup	Corn Grits
1 cup	Quick Oats
1 cup	Powdered Milk
1 cup	Shredded Wheat (3 Large Biscuits)
1/4 cup	Raw Wheat Germ
3 tbsp	Poppy Seed
1 tsp	Plain Gelatin
½ tsp	Avian Vitamin Powder

Mix all ingredients together; add 1 to 3 rounded tablespoons to one mashed large hard-boiled egg along with one small shredded carrot.

Pudding for Canary Nestlings

Everyone loves pudding- even canaries! This should not be fed until chicks are older than four days due to the sugar content.

3	Large Eggs, beaten
1 can	Carrot Juice
1/4 cup	Wheat Germ Flakes
1 tbsp	Sunflower or Olive Oil
1 tbsp	Honey
1/4 tsp	Salt
½ tsp	Avian Vitamin Powder
½ tsp	Brewer's Yeast

Combine ingredients just to boiling and then remove from stove. Add 1 cup Instant Cream of Wheat or Instant Cream of Rice. Add 1 tablespoon of gelatin softened in 1/4 cup of cold water. Refrigerate. Give birds what they will eat in a 2-hour period.

Pudding can be cut into serving size pieces, wrapped and frozen. Thaw before serving.

Quick Eggfood

Crumble six large biscuits of shredded wheat (2 cups). Pour a can of carrot juice over it and allow to stand for ten to fifteen minutes. Add enough yellow corn meal and rolled oats to make a dry crumbly mixture. Set aside. Mash six hard-boiled eggs and 1 teaspoon of Vionate vitamin powder together. Mix the shredded wheat mixture and the boiled egg mixture together until moist and crumbly.

My Nestling and Molting Eggfood Formula

This is a complicated formula and one which is expensive to make, yet I have had great success with it so I continue to use it. This is served dry in the breeding cage at all times in addition to the regular seed mix and pellets. When chicks hatch the dry mix is combined with boiled egg, soak seed, and finely chopped carrot and broccoli. Feed a small amount of the moistened mixture two to three times per day with the remaining feedings being greens, moistened shredded wheat, boiled egg yolk, high protein cornbread or other suitable food.

I never measure anything so I have included ingredients and not measurements. I make enough for the entire breeding season a month before breeding season begins and so the formula remains the same throughout the breeding season despite the lack of measuring.

These items make up the bulk of the mixture:
Coarsely Ground Corn Meal
Corn Grits
High Protein Soybean Meal or Soy Isolate Powder
Oatmeal- Quick Cooking, Old Fashioned or Steel Cut
Shredded Wheat (if you skip any ingredient, don't skip the shredded wheat!)
Whole Wheat/Oatmeal Bread Crumbs
Mixed Baby Cereal

These make up a smaller portion:
Fine Sunflower Chips
Untoasted (raw) Wheat Germ
Textured Vegetable Protein
Nutritional Yeast Flakes
Wheat Flakes (like rolled oats, but made from wheat)
Soy Baby Formula or Ground Pretty Bird Breeder Pellets

Little is needed:
Anise Seed
Poppy seed
Thistle
Hulled Sesame Seed

Very little is needed:
Spirulina powder (a very small quantity goes a long way)

All of these ingredients are mixed together, placed in freezer bags and stored in the freezer to prevent the soybean meal and wheat germ from becoming rancid. Enough for just a few days feeding is kept out at room temperature- this thaws very quickly so it can be placed in the cages while still frozen if you are feeding it dry. A sprinkling of a nutritional supplement such as Avian Advantage and a liberal quantity of bee pollen granules is served over the top of this mixture.

This mixture can also be placed in a food processor with several boiled eggs with eggshells intact (about 1/4 cup dry mix to each egg) and whirred about for a few seconds to make a moist, crumbly textured eggfood the birds absolutely love. Placing both the eggs and dry mix in the food processor together and mixing for a brief period prevents the mixture from becoming an unpalatable mass. Birds will refuse to eat eggfood which has been over processed.

Costs of this mixture can be kept down by purchasing the ingredients through bulk food stores and online at www.bulkfoods.com. I have also been able to find some things for very reasonable prices at a local mill, which sells coarse grits ground by special request for a wonderfully low price. Other items can be located at natural food stores which sell items in bulk. The Avian Advantage is rather pricy for a large number of birds- you may substitute with the human version which comes in a much larger package for about the same price. This supplement contains omega-3 oils and gives a very nice glossy sheen to the feathers.

As one can imagine, this nestling food can quickly lead to an alarming level of obesity in birds which are not feeding babies so care must be taken to feed this rich eggfood sparingly outside of the breeding season. Babies fed this are very nicely fattened prior to weaning and seem to wean without some of the problems with weight loss which can sometimes occur. As a molting supplement a small amount of this is fed to birds two or three times a week (less if the cornbread is fed).

Recipe for Nestling & Molting Cornbread

This bread can be crumbled and placed in the freezer to keep it fresh. Remove the quantity needed for a couple of days' worth of feeding and store in a sealed container in the refrigerator. It can be mixed with finely chopped carrot, broccoli or other fresh vegetables.

This is a good nestling food to use when one cannot be home to change the eggfood every three to four hours as there is no boiled egg in it which can spoil. The birds seem to relish it and feed it very well.

This is fed every day to breeding birds with babies and three to four times per week to molting birds. Optional ingredients can be added according to the bird's needs- for example, add calendula petals to the bread when the birds are molting and calcium powder when the birds are breeding.

This cornbread is very high in vegetable proteins which do not seem to be as likely to produce gout as do animal-based proteins, such as egg. This bread is fattening, so feed it in moderation!

The most important thing with this recipe is to maintain the proper proportion of dry to wet ingredients. Too much water will produce a moist, clumpy mixture which the birds do not care for.

Basic Ingredients

8 boxes of cornbread mix
8 large eggs
Sufficient baby food to moisten mixture (about 6 large jars). Usually carrot or sweet potato. If
      possible, use the food for older babies as this is thicker and contains less water.
Powdered avian vitamins (according to package directions)

Optional Additions

Texturized Vegetable Protein (TVP)
Soy Isolate Protein Powder
Spirulina
Rolled or Steel Cut Oatmeal
Fine Sunflower Chips
Wheat Grass Powder
Poppy Seed
Ground Flaxseed
Calendula Petals
Calcium Powder OR Baked, Finely Crushed Eggshells

Directions

Preheat oven to 400 degrees. Grease two 11" x 7" baking pans and set aside.

Empty cornbread mix into a large mixing bowl, add vitamin powder and optional dry ingredients. Mix thoroughly. Make a depression in the center of the dry mixture and add eggs and baby food. Mix together just until dry ingredients are moistened.

Turn the cornbread batter into baking pans, dividing mixture evenly between the two pans. Bake for approximately 40 minutes (exact baking time varies- begin checking for doneness after about 35 minutes). Cornbread is done when the mixture springs back lightly in the center when touched.

Allow to cool completely in the pans before cutting.

Health Issues

No advice can replace the training and experience of an experienced avian veterinarian. However, cases do arise in which one cannot access a vet with experience in treating small birds in a timely manner. In these cases, a certain amount of logical problem solving will frequently go a long way toward treating a health-related problem. The following pages are a collection of scraps of information I have gleaned from various sources and a few solutions which have in my own experience been useful.

This information should not be viewed as an exhaustive treatment of a particular issue, but a general guide.

Three things should remain foremost in one's mind when treating illness in canaries. First, do no harm. Taking a shotgun approach can cause more harm than good and if by chance one of the treatments works, one is left with the question of which treatment or combination of treatments was effective. Second, always start with the simplest causes and treatments and work out from there. Third, the old adage that an ounce of prevention is worth a pound of cure is absolutely correct and the importance of prevention cannot be overstated.

The single treatment that one can apply to any illness is supportive care- providing warmth, reducing stress and isolating the bird from other birds. Often this will be all that is required to allow a basically healthy bird to recover.

Signs of Illness
- Behavior changes such as sleeping more often or being less active than normal. (This change in behavior is normal during the molt.)
- Appetite changes- eating more or less than usual
- Weight changes
- Change in droppings- becoming looser, changing color or reduction in number. Fewer droppings can be one of the first signs that a bird's appetite is off.
- Increased drinking of water not explained by hot weather, increased exercise, or eating salty foods or those high in water content such as greens, cucumber or watermelon.
- "Fluffed up" appearance
- Prolonged molt or absence of molt (unhealthy birds will not molt), ragged or sparse-looking feathers, bare areas where feathers do not regrow
- Loss of song or hoarseness
- Sneezing, coughing, labored breathing, tail bobbing up and down with each breath
- Nasal discharge

- Eye discharge or swollen eyelid
- Favoring a foot or leg
- Swellings or growths
- Sitting drooped on perch or sitting on the floor of the cage
- Droppings stuck to the bird's vent area

Behavior of Sick Birds

- It is the nature of birds to mask illness as long as possible. Often a bird will seem to suddenly sicken and die when in fact it has been ill for some time. For this reason it is very important to watch birds closely- if they seem to eat but few seeds are actually being hulled they may be only simulating feeding behavior!
- Once a bird begins to look drowsy all the time or very lethargic, quits eating, sits on the bottom of his cage puffed up, or looks feeble and rundown it is often too late.

Stress

- One of the most important causes of disease in canaries- and one of the least understood by many pet owners- is stress. Transporting, catching, overcrowding, chilling, being placed in a drafty location and poor nutrition are all stressors which can lead to illness. Any steps which can be taken to reduce stress on a bird will be beneficial- darkening a room and removing perches from a cage will minimize the stress of capture, for example.

Legs and Feet

- Birds stand on their feet all of their lives so it should come as no surprise that their feet can be the focal point of a large variety of problems. Often these problems are preventable- such as improper perching or poor sanitation.
- Providing birds with oval perches as well as rounded ones can provide some relief for birds with sore feet. Perches should be provided which do not permit birds to wrap their toes around them completely and providing perches with a variety of diameters permits birds to adequately exercise these important parts of their bodies.
- Birds which have been banded with closed bands sometimes experience problems with them which may include irritation caused by a rough surface within the band; debris caught between the band and the leg; the band becoming caught up on some object; or allergic reactions to the metal in the band. I routinely advise buyers who purchase birds for pets to either allow me to remove the band before they take the bird or at the least to have the bands removed at the first sign of problems. Bands can be removed with a band cutting tool, although this can be dangerous as a nick in a leg artery can easily cause the bird to bleed to death. Veterinarians can quickly and easily do this for a pet owner.
- One of the worst band-related problems I have seen was in a bird I had sold the

previous year. Late one Friday evening I received a call from the bird's owner who told me that the bird's leg had become swollen around the band. When she brought the bird to my home, it became apparent that this was not a problem of recent development- the bird's leg was hugely swollen and covered in crusty pus. The owner informed me that the bird had always picked at its band, which indicated that something had been irritating the leg for some time. Soaking the leg in warm water removed the crusts, but it was determined that the band had to be removed- no easy task as the band was firmly embedded in the flesh of the leg. After considerable effort, the band was removed but the bird began to bleed profusely which necessitated cauterization of the wound. The owner was advised to take the bird to a veterinarian first thing on Monday morning. Two courses of antibiotics were required to resolve the infection in the leg which had begun with irritation from the band. Amazingly, the little bird survived with only the loss of two toes and part of a third toe and is doing well. This entire problem could have been avoided had the band been removed at the first sign of problems.

- Male birds in breeding condition often "feed" their bands and food can build up between the leg and the band which can cause irritation. Birds can also develop a compulsive band picking habit.

- Bands should always remain loose- tight bands interfere with blood flow.

- Bumblefoot is a condition in which the bottom of a foot becomes infected. This can affect both feet or only one. Initially the skin appears slightly reddened and inflamed and the bird may or may not be seen to favor the foot. Left alone, eventually the bird's feet swell and an open sore develops which breaks open, crusts over and scabs, and then breaks open again. Blood may be seen on the perches, but often there are no obvious signs until the bird begins favoring a foot or quits perching and is found sitting on the cage floor. For this reason, birds should be examined regularly and the feet inspected to ensure that they are healthy. The causes of bumblefoot are most commonly unsanitary conditions or the use of sandpaper-covered perches and cage liners, although obesity or poor nutrition can also cause the problem.

- Treating bumblefoot requires strict adherence to good sanitation. Padding the perches can help as well. Generally topical antibiotic ointment is needed to treat the wound and further antibiotic therapy may be needed as well in situations where the topical treatment fails to resolve the problem.

- Another common problem in canaries is scaly legs, which is the excessive buildup or thickening of the outer horny layer of skin on the legs. Mites are sometimes involved but as canaries age their legs also tend to become scalier, which is normal and does not require treatment unless the scales become excessive.

- If scaly leg mites are involved, they can be treated with Scatt or ivermectin and the scales covered with a thin layer of olive or mineral oil daily until the scales can gently be removed. Soaking the legs in warm water will also help loosen scales. The scales are ready to be removed when they are easy to remove with a fingernail gently pushed up under the edge of a scale- this indicates that fresh skin has had a chance to grow underneath. Removing scales too soon will result in open wounds which may bleed and become infected (not to mention the fact that it is very painful to the bird).

- An old remedy for scaly leg mite is to lightly cover the legs in olive or mineral oil- this is thought to suffocate the mites living under the scales. Be sure not to use too much oil- if it gets on the feathers and exposes bare skin, birds may become chilled.

- Gout is a disease in which the kidneys are unable to efficiently remove waste products from the bloodstream. Typically gout presents in canaries as warm, reddened, swollen legs and feet and is a problem more common in obese birds and those which are fed an overly rich diet. As there is no treatment for this problem, one can only prevent it by being careful to avoid feeding too much high-protein and fatty foods such as egg, song food and similar items- especially to birds confined in small cages. Exercise is a good preventative but no substitute for proper management of the diet. Once a bird has had gout, it is more susceptible to developing it again.

- This said, I have never seen a hen afflicted with gout while feeding babies even when fed very high protein foods- the most common gout victim (and they are victims because gout can be crippling) is a bird who is housed in a smallish cage and fed lavishly.

- Tassel-foot is a condition in which infestation by a mite causes a growth which resembles fringe or tassels to appear on the sides of the feet. This growth can cause bleeding. As for all other mite infestations, ivermectin is an effective treatment.

- Occasionally birds will get a very small fiber or a hair wrapped around a toe- this will cause the toe to swell and become necrotic due to decreased blood flow. Eventually the toe will self-amputate. This can best be avoided by keeping small threads (especially those made of synthetic fibers) away from birds and carefully examining the feet of any bird seen to be favoring a foot. A magnifying glass is sometimes needed to see the fiber.

- In very young birds, a deformity called slipped claw is sometimes found. The back toe comes up through the front toes and makes it very difficult and sometimes impossible for the bird to perch. This is not a genetic condition but is instead most frequently caused by injury in the nest and usually when the nest contains only one or two chicks. To prevent this from occurring, place clear eggs or plastic "dummy" eggs in the nest with the chick to support it and to protect it from being squashed by the hen when she sits on it. If a baby has developed a slipped claw, the earlier you intervene the better. Gently stretch the toe back and fix it in the proper position by wrapping a very thin piece of paper tape around the back toe and- using the leg as a splint- fix the toe back, being sure not to wrap the ball of the foot and allowing the very end of the toe to remain free. The bird should be able to perch with the tape on its foot. As the muscles develop, the tape will need to be adjusted. The bird will chew on the bandage- watch the bird to make sure it is not removed. Treatment can take from weeks to months depending on how soon the condition has been caught.

Loss of Song

- Loss of song is often a sign of poor health as young, healthy male canaries will sing given appropriate environmental conditions such as adequate lighting, housing and diet.
- The single most common cause of failure to sing- outside of actually being a hen- is molting. The majority of male birds will not sing during the molt and those who do usually sing more softly and quietly than usual.
- The drive to sing is hormonal- male canaries sing only when testosterone levels are normal. For this reason older birds will sometimes sing less often as they age. As birds come into breeding condition, they will sing more often and more loudly. Male birds caged with a hen will often quit singing as the purpose of song is to attract a mate by announcing one's vigor and fitness to breed. When two males are caged together, often a less dominant male will cease to sing in acknowledgment of the dominance of the other male.
- Almost anything that can affect a bird's wellbeing can lead to loss of song as well. To name only a few of the most common things which cause birds to quit singing- air sac mites, sore throat, respiratory infections, external parasite infestations, intestinal complaints, over breeding, and poor nutrition.

Feather Loss

- Baldness can be caused by such a variety of things that each situation must be addressed on its own merits- generalizations about the condition can lead one off track and result in weeks or months lost in providing ineffective treatments.
- Canaries which are not molting and are losing feathers from their head and neck area may be deficient in Vitamin D. Some finches with feather loss are deficient in iodine, but iodine deficiency is not a frequent problem in canaries. If the problem is vitamin deficiency, the addition of a high quality vitamin supplement should readily solve the problem.
- Be sure the source of the problem is not lice or mites. Mites cause intense irritation and birds can pluck their own feathers in an effort to relieve the itching. If the problem is parasites, a round of ivermectin will take care of the problem. This is available from avian veterinarians or from ABBA seed. (Over dosages can result in death, so be very careful.).
- Skin irritations can lead to a bird literally rubbing its feathers off. An ointment for soothing skin irritations such as Bag Balm (originally sold for using on irritated cow's udders) can be applied with a cotton swab on the bald patches. Be careful not to get any of the salve on feathers as it will mat them down and can cause chilling.
- Some viral infections can also cause a similar problem. Balding caused by viral infections can only be treated by boosting the immune system- good nutrition and maintaining a low-stress environment are key. Affected birds must be segregated and careful attention paid to sanitation to prevent the spread of disease.

- Be sure your birds are not plucking each other. An aggressive bird can easily pluck several birds bald in a very short time.
- Molting does not cause bald patches because the new feathers coming in are what push the old feathers out.
- Generally, feathers will grow out fine after the next molt. If the bird appears to be in good overall health and free of parasites, just wait and see what happens after the next molt. At any rate, even if the problem is resolved new feathers will not appear until the bird molts again.

Diarrhea and Loose Stools

- Before commencing to treat diarrhea, be sure that it exists. A few loose stools is not cause for panic. If the bird seems to be in general good health, is singing and is not acting any differently than it usually does chances are good that it is a passing episode and the bird will be fine.
- Loose stools are a symptom rather than an illness in itself. Diarrhea can be caused by diet, stress, bacterial or viral infections, parasites . . . Do not assume the cause to be bacterial and begin giving antibiotics right away- remember to start by addressing possible causes that are the simplest to correct and proceeding from there.
- Nervousness or stress due to changes in the environment can cause a bird to pass watery stools.
- After nervousness or stress, the most common cause of loose stools is feeding too much green food or fruit. Birds which are not accustomed to eating fruits and vegetables regularly will often gorge themselves when offered a large amount- offer only small tidbits and gradually increase portions until the bird becomes used to eating them.
- Large stools are common in hens while they are sitting due to the fact that they hold their stools while in the nest and leave it infrequently. As long as the droppings are firm, there is no cause for concern.
- Don't feed iceberg lettuce to birds- it is devoid of nutrition, containing mostly fiber and water. Feeding it will result in loose stools.
- Foods high in salt will produce diarrhea. While all living things require a certain amount of salt in their diets to live, birds are not able to handle much more than very, very small quantities- too much can be fatal. One overlooked source of salt is softened water- if you use a water softener and do not have a tap for drinking water which has been bypassed from the softener, supply purified bottled water for your birds.
- Wash all produce thoroughly to remove chemical residues, bacterial contaminants and other potential problems. Give fresh food such as greens, broccoli and carrots a short soak in water to which cider vinegar has been added.
- Do not leave fresh food in the cage for too long- a good rule of thumb to use is to leave fresh food before the birds no longer than you would leave your own food out.
- Wash all water and food dishes with dishwashing soap and sterilize with a 1:9

bleach/water solution. Rinse the bleach solution off the dishes thoroughly. Maintaining clean water dishes is vital- birds frequently fill their water dishes with bits of food and all sorts of other things. Change water whenever it becomes dirty and provide only fresh, clean water in clean cups, drinkers, or bottles. All treatment suggestions presume that good hygiene is being maintained!

- Withhold eggfood, fruit and green food and feed a half-teaspoonful of poppy seed until the stools firm up. Often the poppy seed will resolve a simple bout of loose stools.
- Black tea made normal strength and cooled to room temperature can sometimes relieve diarrhea.
- If the diarrhea is unresolved by the poppy seed or returns when the poppy seed is discontinued, switch the bird to bottled water. Often "city water"- water which has been chemically treated with chlorine and other substances- can irritate a bird's bowels; some birds are more sensitive than others. Well water can also cause problems because it can sometimes harbor bacteria to which small birds are less resistant than humans.
- Electrolyte solutions for infants such as Pedialyte can help a bird maintain proper electrolyte balance during periods of diarrhea. There is now a powdered form on the market which is more economical since the bottles for infants are much larger than needed to treat a single bird. The powdered form is sold as a box of individual packets and can be stored for some time at room temperature and probably indefinitely if frozen.
- Add a few drops of cider vinegar to the bird's drinking water. The actual amount will depend on the preexisting acidity of your water and the size of the drinker or cup. Usually a few healthy drops in a half cup or so of water is sufficient. The reasoning behind this is that it will acidify the gut, easing digestive disturbances.
- Other breeders have had good results from the use of probiotics- which are thought to restore levels of "good" bacteria to the gut- though some scientific studies have indicated that probiotics are less effective or even completely ineffective in canaries. Some studies have suggested that the reason probiotics appears to be effective in canaries is due to the product acidifying the gut, which one would think could be effected less expensively by using cider vinegar. Personally, I use probiotics infrequently and only after birds have received antibiotic treatment.
- Antibiotics can be effective in cases of diarrhea which resist all other treatments. Some antibiotics can be purchased at pet and farm supply stores. For treating large numbers of canaries antibiotics such as Tylan and terramycin, which are sold for use in poultry, can be used. Dosing is tricky as amounts are generally provided for mixing large amounts of solution in strengths appropriate for chickens, ducks, and turkeys- not for canaries. Unless you have experience administering such treatments to canaries, don't try to figure out the dosing yourself- see an avian vet.
- If all else has failed to cure the diarrhea, a visit to an avian veterinarian who can perform tests on the bird's droppings should be made to determine the cause.

Colds, Asthma, Wheezing, and Other Respiratory Ailments

- Some asthma can be hereditary, but the majority of respiratory ailments are caused by keeping birds in improper conditions or contagious illness.
- Keeping birds in damp environments will lead to respiratory problems. If birds are kept in a basement, using a dehumidifier may be necessary during summer months.
- Use of an air purifier will assist in preventing irritation of birds' lungs by airborne pollution. This is especially true during the molt, when the dust created by the molting process can become very thick. (As always, good sanitation will prevent a great many problems.)
- Do not introduce birds into your bird room without an appropriate isolation period- bird rooms have been devastated by seemingly healthy new birds that carried illnesses.
- Moldy seed (or mold in the environment) can sometimes cause a fungal infection in the throat. A few drops of tincture of iodine in the drinking water have been recommended as a possible treatment. A local breeder once had a terrible outbreak of respiratory illness in her aviary- upon investigation, it was discovered that the dehumidifier used in the bird room was full of mold. When this was addressed, the birds began to recover.
- Birds showing symptoms of respiratory problems (sneezing, labored breathing, wheezing, etc.) should be fed easily digested, high energy foods such as oats to prevent weight loss.
- A couple of drops of whiskey added to a sick bird's drinking water have reportedly cured colds according to a number of old canary care books. The same thing has been used to treat pain by breeders in the past.
- Wheezing is sometimes caused by air sac mites, which can be eliminated by administering ivermectin or other commercially available medications. Be aware that sometimes when a bird is severely afflicted, treatment can be fatal. Doing nothing will be fatal as well so treatment should be given. Air sac mites are highly contagious, especially between parent and baby birds. High-pitched wheezing- which is often described as a "clicking sound"- in apparently healthy birds at night should cause one to suspect air sac mites. Other symptoms include loss of song, weight loss, sneezing, tail bobbing, and open-mouthed breathing.

Contagious Illness in the Aviary

- Contagious illness can be one of the greatest threats to a flock. For this reason, never purchase a bird which appears to be at all ill. Birds are masters at masking illness- often they only begin to appear ill shortly before death. If a bird looks sick, do not bring it home! Do not buy any other bird from the dealer offering the sick bird, either- besides the fact that other apparently healthy birds may also be carrying illness, anyone selling sick-looking birds is untrustworthy.
- All birds should be quarantined before introduction to the flock. Most bird experts suggest a thirty-day quarantine during which a bird should be kept in a completely

separate portion of the home and strict hygiene maintained.

- I personally house new birds in a cage in a corner of my birdroom and treat them immediately for parasites with ivermectin and a small drop of Frontline 0.29% spray on the back of the neck or the preen gland. Their dishes and perches are kept separate and I wash and sterilize my hands after caring for them. If within a few weeks the bird is healthy, active, and shows no signs of illness the bird is placed in the flight with the rest of my flock. I do not, however, purchase birds from pet stores or at bird fairs- only from breeders with good reputations. I do not buy a lot of birds nor do I buy from people who raise birds only for profit- I only purchase birds from breeders who also exhibit and thus tend to manage their birds accordingly. I have no problem with leaving a breeder's home empty handed. If you have any doubts at all, leave a bird where it is. You only invite grief into your home if you buy a bird covered in mites, showing symptoms of illness or generally looking bedraggled and out of sorts.

- A breeder of my personal acquaintance purchased a pair of lizard canaries at a bird fair. One glance at this pair of birds was enough to indicate that the birds had rarely been given a chance to bathe and certainly their diet had been less than ideal for the better part of their young lives. Despite my advice to avoid these birds, this breeder purchased the pair and brought them home to share a room with her other birds. She spent months trying to rid the birds of the mites they were covered in (and all of her other birds as well since the birds were happy to share their mites with their new roommates) and attempting to nurse these birds back to health with no success. The birds died despite all of her efforts within six months of purchase.

- Hygiene is important but not the only factor in a bird's health. Many experienced canary breeders will tell you that a bird needs some exposure to germs to develop resistance to infection. This is to a certain extent true, but maintaining basic cleanliness goes a very long way in preventing illness. That said, one does not need to sterilize every surface in the birdroom every week as some have suggested- a basic weekly wipe down of surfaces such as cages, walls and flooring, etc. is sufficient. I do, however, believe that clean perches, food and water dishes, and cage papers are very important.

- When an epidemic occurs in a flock, the most important thing to do is to immediately separate all sick birds from healthy ones. Sterilize everything with a 1:9 solution of bleach and water. If the disease is virulent and cannot be contained (birds continue to sicken and die) contact an avian veterinarian and arrange for an examination of the sick birds. Sometimes sacrificing a bird for a post mortem exam can save a flock.

- Unfortunately, sometimes even a well-qualified veterinarian cannot say for certain what an illness is and all treatments prove futile. In such cases, one may have to euthanize all sick birds to protect the rest of the flock. In my personal experience and from stories I have gathered from other breeders veterinarians are often at a loss when it comes to illnesses in canaries and even hundreds of dollars worth of tests can leave one with no clear answers. One has a duty to the remaining healthy birds to protect them from illness.

Internal and External Parasites

- Parasites are also discussed in other sections within this chapter.
- The Northern Fowl Mite has been found on many species of birds (including canaries) and on rats, mice and humans. However, fertile populations have only been found on birds. These mites normally never leave the host but can survive off the host for up to two months. Signs of heavy mite infestations can include blackened feathers- especially in the vent area. A sign of infestation in the birdroom can include buildup of black droppings in cracks and crevices near cages. Look in the area of the spring on clothespins used to hold rope perches- this is a favorite place for mites to hide.
- Red mites breed most heavily during warm weather and more slowly during colder weather. They are nocturnal feeders and hide under cage papers and in cracks and crevices and lay eggs there as well. Even after birds are removed, infestations can remain for six months.
- Most breeders use carbaryl powder (one brand name is Sevin) between the nest liner and the nest the hen builds to prevent and treat mites, which can drive hens off the nest or weaken and kill chicks. I have for several years used a less expensive product with the same ingredients made for treating ticks and fleas on dogs called Happy Jack. It comes in a much smaller container from which the powder can be sprinkled into the nest liner without any difficulty and a single container has lasted me for four years and probably has another three years of product left in it.
- Carbaryl can also be sprinkled under the cage papers in flight cages to prevent mites seeking refuge there.
- Be aware that pest strips must be aired out for several days before placing them in the aviary. A local breeder lost many birds once after hanging up an unaired pest strip.
- Ivermectin treats the broadest range of parasites- external mites including scaly leg, red, and fowl; air sac mites; tracheal mites; and intestinal worms. Ivermectin is available through veterinarians or from farm supply stores.
- Administration of Ivermectin- 1 cc of 1% ivermectin solution per 32 oz water is the dosage recommended by Dr. Abbate of Abba seed. DO NOT GIVE THE <u>UNDILUTED</u> 1% SOLUTION ORALLY. Abba seed has developed the easiest method of using ivermectin to treat a large number of birds that I have found- a bottle of ivermectin is sold by ABBA seed which is added to one gallon of distilled water. Birds are given the water as their sole source of water for an entire day and then treatment is repeated again fourteen days later. Leftover solution can be refrigerated and saved for the second treatment. Ivermectin treats internal and external parasites. Since the only time I ever bring birds into my birdroom is during the fall, birds are treated one time per year before breeding season with ivermectin. Many breeders refuse to use ivermectin sooner than a month or so before breeding commences, but I have used it right into breeding season with no problems. WARNING: This is a very powerful parasiticide and care must be used when administering it. I have never lost a bird due to treatment with ivermectin, but I have heard of other breeders who have.

- Dr. Abbate's article regarding proper administration of ivermectin can be found on the Abba website at www.abbaseed.com.
- Another method of ivermectin administration in drinking water is to use Ivomec Sheep Drench, .08% formula. This is a water-soluble formula and can be used in either drinking water or in the bath. The usual dosage is 20 ml .08% ivermectin to one liter of fresh water. This treatment is provided as the sole source of drinking water for one day; the water is emptied into baths for the birds to bathe in the next day and repeated again in 14 days. The .08% formula is not as strong as the 1% solution and less likely to cause serious side effects.
- Ivermectin injectable Cattle/Swine 1% formula is not water soluble and floats on the top of water. This can lead to overdosing and death.
- I have used ivermectin paste (a small portion the size of the tip of a toothpick is placed into the bird's beak or under the wing where the wing meets the body), but have had better results with less effort with the water administration method.
- Some breeders recommend fogging the birdroom with pyrethrum spray once a month. All doors and windows must be sealed to permit proper penetration of the spray into the nooks and crannies of the room so mites hiding there will be killed.
- A breeder of my personal acquaintance experienced a terrible mite infestation which he could not bring under control. Finally in desperation he took a 32-ounce spray bottle and poured 1 tablespoon of liquid Sevin in it followed by sufficient warm water to fill the bottle. He sprayed all his birds, the cages and the rest of the room with this mixture just before the lights went out for the evening. Despite staying awake all night worrying about the birds, in the morning they were all alive and healthy. This remedied the existing mite problem and repeating this treatment once per month has prevented the recurrence of new mite infestations.

Emergencies
- Cautery is occasionally required to stop bleeding- it is a remedy for a desperate situation in which one has no other choice to prevent a bird from bleeding to death. I have used it on legs, toes, and nails to stop profuse bleeding when all other means were ineffective. I would hesitate to use cautery on other parts of the body, especially feathered areas or on the head.
- Before using cautery, other methods such as using applying gentle pressure and elevating the limb should be tried. For bleeding toenails, quick stop powder is usually effective but rarely the bleeding from a broken toenail is profuse and the powder is ineffective. Heat a thin piece of metal such as the tines of a fork or the metal portion of a vegetable peeler in the flame of a match or over the burner of a gas stove. (Using the flame of a candle generally results in large amounts of soot deposited on the metal and thus all over the wound- cleaning the soot cannot be done as it cools the metal.) The metal should be as hot as possible. Touch the heated metal to the wound- this will burn the flesh black. Repeat as necessary until bleeding stops. Birds will appear to be in

shock for some time and will likely refuse to perch. Place the bird in a hospital cage and treat as for any illness with gentle warmth, easy to digest foods and quiet.

Breeding

Breeding Success- The Triad of Genetics, Lighting, and Diet

Good breeding results rely on a wide array of factors of which the most important are genetics, lighting, and diet.

For novice breeders, the issue of genetics often receives the briefest consideration when breeding canaries; even experienced breeders of show birds often consider this subject only as far as it pertains to the inheritance of song and physical traits. This can happen to the detriment of equally important traits such as personality, breeding tendencies, and overall health and vigor. Many potential problems can be avoided by understanding that good breeding encompasses much more than song and conformation, although these are without a doubt vital.

Most breeders of show quality song canaries look to those characteristics for which a breed is shown to determine how to set up their pairs of birds and fail to consider personality traits such as steadiness or nervousness. If a bird has a tendency to be nervous (which it may very well have inherited from its parents), training that bird to be steady in the show cage will be more difficult, if not impossible. The bird will be less able to cope with the stresses of showing and will present the breeder with more problems during the show season.

Sometimes this is not the case- the bird (or the hen's father or brothers) is very steady in the shows and does very, very well. Of course, the breeder wishes to get babies from this line. Unfortunately, the line of birds does not breed well- producing small clutches or weak babies, feeding poorly, proving to be very nervous in the breeding cage . . . What should a breeder do- produce high quality birds and deal with the stress of a breeding season filled with problems or compromise on quality and produce a line of birds with better breeding behaviors? The two goals are not mutually exclusive- one can accomplish both goals if one proceeds very carefully.

American Singer canaries are noted for being good breeders and excellent parents, but as lines are bred closer and closer for song characteristics often these traits are lost. Without a doubt the song in the American Singer canary must come first, followed by conformation- without these things an American Singer canary is little different from a common "kitchen" canary. However, within the group of individual birds with good song and conformation there will be those with better and worse personality and breeding traits. The key to any breeding program is to ruthlessly select only the best for breeding, resisting the desire to keep individuals who fail to meet the standards you look for.

One example I have had in my bird room is a hen that has an outstanding background with show winning males all the way back on both sides of her pedigree. Unfortunately, this hen is vicious to her fellow flight mates and must be kept separately to prevent the other birds from being plucked and harassed. She attacked several mates offered her but finally accepted a male, built a nest, laid and sat well, fed well and the five chicks fledged perfectly. One day I discovered that the hen had plucked every single one of the babies nearly bald within the space of two hours despite having ample nesting materials including white toilet paper and the other odds and ends with which most hens are delighted.

I could simply continue to breed this hen, pulling her out of the breeding cage before her chicks fledge and leaving the father in the cage to feed. However, she might pass this trait onto her babies and I could end up with a room filled with birds with antisocial traits. I have been in such bird rooms and they are not happy places- an aviary filled with fighting birds means that a breeder must always be on guard to protect the more docile and help the injured. In addition, birds which are watching to make sure they aren't going to be attacked are not practicing their songs or developing healthy, lustrous plumage so the entire aviary suffers. At seven months of age, this hen's chicks are frequently fighting with their fellows and each other- they are beginning to sing beautifully, though. Because of the quality of the song and pedigree, I will select the least antisocial of the nest mates and breed it into a line with more easygoing personalities. Despite the hen's pedigree I will not breed her again for any reason!

I also had this hen's brother, which had a beautiful song and did not seem to have any of the nasty behaviors of the sister as he got along well with other birds and with every hen with which I used him. However, when left in a breeding cage to help out a hen with seven fertile eggs, he turned out to be an egg eater who ate every single egg in one day. This will certainly be a line of birds which bears close watching during breeding season.

There will always be an individual who pops up with these sorts of traits regardless, but if the breeder refuses to breed them they will be the exception rather than the norm.

On the other end of the spectrum, I have many birds who will happily allow themselves to be harassed to death by nearly every bird in the flight- they are completely passive and bear their plucking with an almost human expression of martyrdom. Of course, this is not acceptable either- a canary needs to have some spirit!

What kind of traits do I select for in hens? One of the most important personality traits I look for in an ideal hen is steadiness- an ability to adapt to changes in her surroundings quickly with a minimum of fuss. I will not tolerate a flaky hen that flies off her nest at the slightest thing. My bird room is managed the same way during breeding season as during the rest of the year- I use a shop vacuum to clean the floor and around the cages, I bump into cage stands, move cages around the room, make as much noise as I need to and turn on the television or radio. People walk through my breeding area whenever they need to do so- family members, friends and strangers. I do not tiptoe around my birds at all! I frequently have hens feed their youngsters while a group of folks conversing in normal voices stands right next to the breeding cage despite all the dire predictions I have read in books on canary breeding.

Can this be done with every hen? No. Some hens just cannot tolerate disturbance during breeding season. Those hens do not remain in my room for long and as a consequence I have a group of really good, reliable hens I can depend on. (First time mothers are always given a second chance unless something especially grievous occurs, though.)

Another important trait to look for in hens is her breeding behavior and production- in young hens, one can often predict their maternal abilities from their mother's history. Good feeding parents generally produce offspring which will also feed well. Certain lines of birds will come into breeding condition earlier or later than other lines and some lines of hens produce more males or more hens than others (sex in birds is determined by the hen, not the male). Ending up a breeding season with too many males or hens can put a serious crimp in even the best planned breeding program, so any tendency to produce too much of either sex should be monitored. Some lines of birds will produce large nests of youngsters while some seem to be genetically programmed to produce just a few youngsters. I know of a very experienced breeder who had a pair that never produced more or less than three eggs a year no matter what was done- only one nest, only three eggs for several years while other pairs in the room routinely produced ten babies in two rounds of five babies each. And the eggs weren't even fertile every year!

The second most important factor in breeding success is lighting management- lighting schedule, length of day, and intensity of lighting. Small birds are very photosensitive and relatively minor changes in their schedule can have a great effect on them.

Lighting management is really very simple when it comes to bringing canaries into condition- gradual increases in length of day and brightness are more effective than sudden jumps. When using artificial lighting, increase the length of day in 15-minute increments once a week until the birds come into condition- the amount of hours will depend on the type of canary with the general rule of thumb being that the smaller the bird, the fewer hours required. Some family lines of birds will come into full breeding condition at 12 hours while some will require up to 14½ hours. I have never provided more than 14 hours of light for my American Singers and they have done very well. Brightness is increased in the bird room by simply using more bulbs- my light fixtures can accept up to four bulbs and I use only one in each fixture for most of the year. During breeding season I use three in each fixture.

One of the greatest mistakes novices make is to fiddle around with the lighting when the birds fail to come into breeding condition quickly enough to suit the breeder. Often they increase the lights too rapidly- "pushing" the canaries to come into condition more quickly than is preferable. The impatient breeder is frequently rewarded with infertile eggs, dead in shell babies, and poor parenting. Sometimes a novice will adjust the number of hours up and down or maintain the same number of hours but change the times . . . the kinds of mischief a novice (or experienced but impatient) breeder can get up to with the lighting is amazing- leave the timer alone once you have the birds at a good breeding condition level- when the birds are finished breeding then you can begin adjusting lights! The birds will do better if you maintain consistency.

As far as times, I maintain my birds on a schedule which is convenient to me. As long as <u>all natural light is blocked</u>, the lights can come on and go off whenever you like. (Converting birds to night shifters is probably not going to work, however.) Some have said that birds must never be kept up past 9 pm, but birds in the wild do that all the time during the summer here in the Midwestern United States and there is no reason the lights could not go off at 10 pm if this is more convenient to your schedule. I have known breeders whose lights come on as early as 4 am, but I prefer to be in the room as soon as the lights come on and so my birds awaken rather later than that. At the peak of breeding season, my lights come on at 7 am and turn off at 9 pm.

The last of the three critical factors involved in successful breeding of canaries is diet. In the past few decades a tremendous amount of scientific data has been released to confuse and befuddle the average breeder and pet owner who wishes to provide his or her birds with proper nutrition. The amount of conflicting information available can quickly overwhelm the most intelligent person and everywhere one turns one will encounter devout believers in this or that feeding program.

The three keys to a good diet are freshness, simplicity, and variety. Whatever you chose to feed your birds must be fresh- seed, pellet, vegetable, or fruit. If something is not fresh enough to put on your own table, don't give it to your birds! Don't purchase seed from stores which don't have a quick turnover in stock- the closer you can get to buying your food directly the manufacturer, the better as it is likely to be fresher. Keep your feeding program simple- a high quality basic canary seed mix supplemented with a small amount of pelleted food should be offered daily. Two to three times a week, a small amount of song food can be provided with Petamine or a similar supplement offered on alternate days.

Birds should receive vegetables and fruits regularly- especially greens and carrots, but they don't need them every day and the food should be offered in small quantities. Healthy birds will come into condition perfectly on this diet without the addition of wheat germ oil, vitamin E, egg food or any of the other artificial methods used to push birds into condition. A small amount of egg food offered once a week or so will not harm the birds, but really is not necessary. If birds require more than this to come into condition, one should wonder if the birds are really as healthy as they ought to be.

Before the widespread usage of vitamin E, breeders in the past brought birds into breeding condition by providing large amounts of greens such as dandelion and chicory in the spring. This is effective as a sudden change in diet can encourage coming into condition quickly. However, pushing birds too quickly- even with "natural foods"- can and will result in the variety of breeding problems previously discussed. Beyond the issue of pushing condition, birds which are well fed all year- not only during the "conditioning period"- will be better breeders as they will be healthier and have greater physical reserves as they enter the breeding season. The focus during the conditioning period should be on a *gradual* increase in nutrition levels and lighting- not on making up for past dietary deficiencies with excessive quantities of "foods good for conditioning". Conditioning really begins in the egg- the bird's health is initially determined by that of its parents; after hatching, the bird must receive proper nutrition at every stage of its life so that it may enter into the breeding season as absolutely healthy as possible.

And lastly, variety is important because nutritional deficiencies are less likely to occur when a varied diet is offered. It is beneficial to purchase two different brands of seed and mix them together to ensure that the birds are receiving a complete seed mix. Offer a variety of fruits and vegetables throughout the week rather than the same thing- my birds receive finely chopped broccoli, shredded carrots, sweet potatoes, greens of all kinds, mint leaves, cucumbers, sliced orange, cantaloupe and berries from my garden as well as wild-harvested (and free from exposure to chemical pesticides or other contaminants) dandelion, chicory, and similar plants. They occasionally receive borage, calendula, cucumber, cantaloupe, watermelon, zucchini, and daylily flowers as well.

With careful attention to genetics, lighting management, and diet one can experience greater success during the breeding season with less effort.

Breeding Overview

Breeding Cycle

A breeding cycle (one nest) for canaries lasts 6 to 8 weeks if everything proceeds without complications.

Care of Birds during the Breeding Season

A regular routine is important during the breeding season- birds must be fed on time every day and good sanitation is more important than ever. A small disturbance in the daily routine may prove quite costly. The number of stories told over the years by breeders who went on vacation and left their breeding birds in the care of another person only to return to disaster are both varied and numerous- even the most well meaning and diligent caretaker can upset the birdroom during this important time.

Breeding Condition

Males usually come into condition before the hens in the same room do. The reason for this that part of a male's reproductive responsibility is to bring the hen into condition by singing lustily and communicating to her that she needs to come into breeding condition as there is a vital, healthy, strong male available for mating. Many experienced breeders blame males for healthy hens which are slow in coming into condition.

One way to slow a hen down who is coming into breeding condition too quickly is to cage her with a male who is not in condition as this will signal to her that there is no suitable mate available. Sometimes hens can become very testy in this situation and will bicker with the male- watch the pair to ensure that the situation does not progress beyond squabbling and no blood is drawn.

The most common thing novice breeders are told to look for to determine a hen's readiness for breeding is tearing paper. This is only one thing hens in condition will do, and it is not the best indicator of breeding condition as hens will sometimes begin to tear paper months before they are completely ready. The best sign to look for is the condition of the hen's vent- when she is in condition her vent will be reddened and appear swollen. Another good sign is when hens squat and raise their tails when males are singing nearby. When these two signs are present, the hen will usually build a nest within a day or so of being paired with a mate. On a few occasions I have seen hens that are in peak condition build a complete nest in less than an hour after being presented with nesting materials!

Other signs of readiness in the hen is restless flying back and forth, calling to males, carrying nesting material and bits of paper towards the back of the beak, increased squabbling in the flight cage, and an overall increased level of activity.

Males in breeding condition sing a louder, harsher song which is referred to as "breeding song" and drop their wings when they sing. Some males may dance on the perch, especially those with more Roller blood in their backgrounds. As males come into breeding condition they become more pugnacious and will sing a type of song I think of as "fighting song"- a harsher, more forcefully delivered song than breeding song- which they use to aggressively declare their superiority when they see another male. All males in breeding condition must be kept separately to prevent serious injury or death.

Different bloodlines of birds come into condition at different times. Some lines will come into condition early while others do so slowly. For this reason, it is often best to avoid introducing too many different bloodlines into one's birdroom.

Problems will only result if the breeder tries to push the birds into condition before they are ready through the use of vitamin E, eggfood, or other dietary supplements. Healthy birds will come into condition without these things and those allowed to come into condition naturally will be more fertile and experience fewer problems throughout the breeding process.

Overall, allowing the hen to decide when breeding season begins is the best decision.

Properly fed and cared-for hens can continue to breed for at least four years, possibly five. Males may retain fertility longer. With both hens and males, fertility tends to decline with age. One should also keep in mind that the average life span for breeders is about five years so if one breeds a hen who is five years old (and many healthy five year old hens do insist on breeding and manage successfully) one needs to have a backup plan in the form of a younger nesting hen to foster eggs or chicks to in case the hen dies. Often old hens who manage successfully through breeding season will die during the molt.

Breeding Records
Poor record keeping during the breeding season will return to haunt you during the show season when you are determining which stock to keep and which to sell.

A 3 in. x 5 in. index card for each pair can be made which contains the following information:

```
Band Number Hen _____        Band Number Male _____

Clutch Number _____
First Egg Laid _____        Number of Eggs Laid _____
Date Set _____    Date to Candle _____    Number of Fertile Eggs _____
Hatch Due Date _____    Hatch Date _____    Number Hatched _____
Band Numbers of Chicks _____
```

Simply attach the index card to the breeding cage with a wooden clothespin and add numbers and dates!

Pairing

Prior to pairing, the birds' nails should be clipped to prevent damage to eggs from occurring. Some breeders who use stud males do not clip the nails of the male. However, any males to be left in the cage to feed should have their nails trimmed.

Some heavily-feathered birds need to be trimmed around the vent to increase contact during copulation. Care must be taken to not clip the "feeler feathers" located at the tip of the vent or birds will not be able to mate successfully. Feather trimming is generally unnecessary with American Singers.

Once in a while a hen will be very determined in her choice of mate- even if she has never been mated before, she may have her mind made up as to which male in the room she is willing to accept. Generally such hens can be coaxed into taking the mate of the breeder's choice but occasionally one encounters a hen that will have none of it. I had a hen who decided that she would have no mate but the one caged above her with another hen. Every male I placed with her came out of the cage worse for the experience- the first male I caged her with had nearly all of his flight and tail feathers pulled in less than ten minutes and none of the other males were any more successful. Finally, I gave in to her and allowed her to mate with the male of her choice. Then I pulled him after sitting her with her eggs and placed the mate of my choice with her to see her through incubation and feeding. She was willing to go a second round with the male who helped her feed the first nest. Another breeder had a pair of birds who bonded so tightly that they never accepted another mate- they even perched close to each other in the walk-in flight during the molt. The breeder wished to mate the hen to different males but she simply would not cooperate. Her mate was placed in the breeding cage next to her so that she could see and hear him while the male the breeder had chosen was placed in the breeding cage with her just before the lights went out in the birdroom for the night. In the morning when the lights came on her mate sang to her and when she squatted to signal her readiness for mating, the male placed in her cage mated her. This is a rather sneaky way to accomplish a chosen pairing, but it was effective. The hen's chosen mate was placed back with her and helped her raise the babies sired by a male of the breeder's choosing.

Truly testy hens can sometimes be bred by allowing the hen to build her nest in a breeding cage and then transferring her to the male's cage for mating. After the birds have mated several times, she can be returned to her cage.

Often the breeder will never witness the birds mating but they will produce fertile eggs. Some birds are simply shy and mate only when the breeder is out of the room. If the pair seems to be getting along and the male is feeding the hen then they are probably mating and they should be fine.

Fertility

Clear eggs occur often early in the breeding season, before birds are really in breeding condition. Hastiness in putting birds together can waste a considerable amount of time and breeders who rush the season can easily find themselves apace with more patient breeders in a story reminiscent of *The Tortoise and The Hare* . . . A breeder of my acquaintance waits until nearly March before putting his birds together, allowing them to come into condition naturally without the use of any breeding stimulants at all except light and comes up with nearly two hundred babies after a single round of nesting every year. Every nest has four or five babies and he experiences very few clear eggs. Other breeders beginning in December have to breed three rounds with the same number of hens to come up with the same results- often finishing the season later than the patient breeder!

Fertility can be affected by unstable perching which does not allow successful copulation. Obesity in either male or hen can also make copulation more difficult and impact fertility.

The time span between mating and the laying of fertile eggs is a matter of debate. Some breeders believe that 24 hours is the minimum period of time and others that four or five days are required between mating and commencement of laying for all eggs to be fertile. One day is cutting it rather fine, but it is possible.

Eggs can continue to be fertile for a considerable time after mating. Anecdotal evidence indicates that fertile eggs have been laid weeks after a hen has mated, although this time span is probably not common.

For all eggs to be fertile, males used for stud should be in the cage at least through the laying of the fourth egg. Males can be run with one hen in the morning and placed with another in the afternoon or left in one hen's cage all day. Hens can sometimes become overly attached to a male and refuse to sit without his presence- with these birds, leaving the male in the breeding cage until the hen has been sitting for several days can help as she is fairly well attached to her duties by this time.

Nesting

The most inexpensive and satisfactory nest liner can be made from several disposable paper coffee filters of a size to fit inside a plastic nest with a half inch or so extra to wrap over the edge of the nest. The coffee filters can be fixed to the nest with masking tape around the nest edge. When the paper becomes soiled, simply tear it off and throw it away!

Provide hens with plenty of suitable material such as sharpie, sisal, jute, etc. to build nests. Many hens seem to prefer light-colored material. Nesting material is readily available online and inexpensive enough that the traditional method of purchasing burlap, washing and bleaching it, cutting it into two-inch squares and separating it for the hens is unnecessary nowadays. I can attest from personal experience that burlap can cause serious problems in modern washing machines and dryers as well if the burlap is not placed inside a pillowcase first! A bag of jute or sharpie nesting material can be purchased for less than $10 and may be enough for a breeding season for a number of pairs.

Providing hens with something soft with which they can line their nests - such as white unscented toilet paper- may prevent the use of a mate's feathers being used as nest lining material.

Hens not quite in full breeding condition may build complete nests and then tear them apart several times. Once hens achieve peak breeding condition they should settle down.

I provide a small plastic nest for hens to build their nests to lay and sit in and change the nest to a larger one made for Border canaries when the chicks are banded. This decreases the likelihood of babies falling from the nest when there are four or more chicks in the nest. In fact, I have not had a single baby fall out of a nest since doing this and I have never had a hen refuse the new nest. It is possible for a hen to refuse the different type of nest, so make sure to have the old one handy just in case.

Eggs

The average clutch is five eggs. An average is just that- the middle number of eggs one can expect a hen to lay. It is perfectly normal for a hen to lay anywhere between one and seven eggs, although even a clutch of eight eggs is not completely unheard of. Clutch size has a number of components- genetics, level of breeding condition, general health, and other issues play interactive roles.

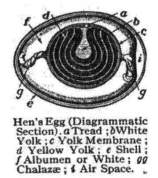

Hen's Egg (Diagrammatic Section). *a* Tread ; *b* White Yolk ; *c* Yolk Membrane ; *d* Yellow Yolk ; *e* Shell ; *f* Albumen or White ; *gg* Chalazæ ; *i* Air Space.

The number of eggs a hen can properly cover depends on the hen's size and the nest she has built. Experienced hens can generally manage to cover more eggs than younger ones.

Laying hens need extra water to produce eggs- make sure that she is supplied with all the water she desires. Watch water bottles and make sure they are functioning properly. Linda Hogan reports that one can predict when a hen will begin to lay by monitoring water intake- a day or two before the first egg is laid the hen will drink substantially more than normal.

Eggs should be pulled from the nest as they are laid and replaced with plastic eggs until the entire clutch is laid to ensure that all chicks will hatch at about the same time and smaller, younger ones will not be trampled or starved by larger, older ones. Even a single day's difference can make a significant difference in a chick's survival chances. Some books recommend replacing the real eggs after the fourth egg is laid, but after having several nests of six or seven fertile eggs, I have come to wait until all the eggs have been laid to avoid problems.

Canary hens cannot count- all a hen will need is a couple of plastic eggs regardless of the number of eggs she lays. Replacing the number of eggs laid with an equal number of dummy eggs is helpful to the absent-minded breeder who cannot remember the number of eggs laid, however!

Eggs pulled from the nests can be stored in a cool area of approximately 50- 60 degrees for seven to ten days after being laid without problems. Hatchability begins to decline after the eggs are a week old by about 1% per day unless storage conditions are ideal, which few breeders are able to provide. Do not stand eggs on the large end- this may rupture the air cell. Lay eggs on their sides in the place they will be stored and turn a quarter or a half turn twice each day they are stored.

A dusting of Sevin powder between the nest liner and the hen's nest will deter mite problems. This can be done when the hen is set on her eggs.

Hens who skip days between laying eggs are generally not in full breeding condition and should be recycled by placing them back in the flight for a couple of weeks. Young hens are more likely to do this than older hens, but some hens will skip-lay every time. Skip laying is probably caused by lack of condition if the hen skips more than a single day, lays bumpy or thin shelled eggs, or just cannot seem to find her "breeding groove." If the hen looks ill she may be egg bound. Should the skip laying hen manage to lay an entire clutch, she will more than likely experience more problems further down the road such as refusing to sit or feed. Eggs can be fostered with another pair.

Humidity is vital to the viability of chicks- maintain a humidity level of a minimum of 40%

when there are eggs in the birdroom. This can be easily accomplished by using a humidifier (more than one if necessary). Failure to maintain proper humidity results in dead in shell and dehydrated chicks who cannot hatch because the membrane inside the shell has dried onto their bodies. To ensure that there is sufficient humidity to allow hatching, permit the hen to bathe the day before eggs are due to hatch. The breeder can also sprinkle or mist the eggs with a small amount of warm water.

Research has shown that each egg receives a small quantity of testosterone from the mother regardless of the chick's sex. This occurs very early in the development of the egg- before fertilization. The testosterone is contained within a layer of cells surrounding the egg yolk. During incubation the testosterone enters the yolk and the chick's bloodstream. The first egg receives the smallest amount and each successive egg a larger one. The last egg may receive as much as twenty times more than the first! For this reason, chicks which hatch from later eggs tend to be more aggressive than their earlier-laid nest mates. Scientists theorize that this assists late hatching chicks to compete with earlier ones. (Of course, when eggs are pulled and set at one time chicks will hatch at roughly the same time.)

The last egg laid tends to have a deeper bluish color compared to the hen's other eggs. The color difference can be subtle, but often it is remarkable. Not all hens will lay blue eggs, but if one is laid it is most likely the last egg of a clutch.

At about seven days, eggs can be candled to check for fertility. Fertile eggs will appear dark when light is shined through them while infertile eggs will appear clear. (Clear eggs are not really clear- a yolk is visible.)

After using a number of different egg candlers, I now candle my eggs with an ordinary flashlight as I have found this to work the best for me. The nest of eggs to be candled is removed from the breeding cage to a darkened room and placed on a roll of masking tape so it will not tip over. The flashlight is stood on its end so that the light shines up toward the ceiling and turned on. Eggs are gently removed from the nest and held over the light from the flashlight. A hand towel which has been placed near the flashlight serves as a soft resting place for the candled eggs and prevents mix-ups with those which have not yet been checked. After all eggs are checked, the nest is replaced and the number of fertile eggs noted on the breeding record attached to the cage.

Candling is a delicate process and great care must be taken- numerous breeders have lost nests filled with eggs by taking this process too casually and failing to give the task their complete attention.

An old repair for small cracks in the shell of an egg is clear nail polish. Several thin coats should be applied as soon as possible after the crack occurs. It does not always work, but it's worth a try as otherwise the chick will certainly die. This will not work if the inner membrane of the egg has been punctured.

If all the eggs in the nest are infertile and the hen is not going to be used as a foster parent, she should be recycled by returning her to the flight cage for a week and a half to two weeks.

It has been written that fertile eggs which are twelve or thirteen days along in their development can survive even if the hen is off of the nest for quite a while. It is thought that the chicks are large enough to keep themselves warm for short periods. Should the hen leave the nest at this stage, transfer the eggs to another nest. I am uncertain about the validity of this assertion, but it certainly would not do to give up hope and throw away the eggs too soon. Should the chicks survive they would likely hatch a day or two later than expected as development would be affected by the lower temperature, even though it was temporary.

Sitting Hens

Sitting hens which are in full breeding condition develop an incubation or brood patch, which is a bare area on the lower abdomen which permits direct contact of the skin with the eggs. Jo Hall wrote in her "Bird Talk From Shady Grove" column for *Cage Bird Magazine* that "before the hen lays her first egg . . . the skin loses its feathers; the outer layers of skin thicken; the blood vessels increase in number and become enlarged; and the spaces between the cells under the skin fill with tissue fluid and remain full during the incubation period." The development of the brood patch is caused by hormones associated with reproduction- thus it is an excellent indicator of good breeding condition.

Sitting hens are funny creatures- some sit their eggs as though their very lives depended on the successful hatching of the eggs beneath them while others shoot off the nest like a rocket every time someone enters the room. Hens of the former variety are generally preferable and will be steadier mothers, provided they are willing to leave the nest to feed once the chicks hatch.

A sitting hen who abandons her nest can sometimes be induced into going back to her nest by removing the nest from the cage and placing the eggs under a foster hen, a hen that has eggs which look very different, or (if you carefully place a small mark on the egg so you can tell the eggs apart) another sitting hen. Leave the nest out of the hen's cage for an hour or so and then replace it in the same location in the cage- including some plastic eggs. More often than not the hen will return to her nest and her eggs can be given back to her. This method was related by Herman Osman in his book *Canary Breeding, Tips and Tricks* and has worked for me.

Hens that push eggs out of the nest may have nests which are too shallow. Making the nest deeper by removing some of the nesting material will remedy this problem.

Many breeders believe that hens are able to sense that eggs are infertile due to a lack of movement or the way that infertile eggs feel differently underfoot. A hen is certainly more likely to deliberately roll an infertile egg out of her nest than a fertile one.

Sitting hens should be provided a nutritious but not overly rich diet since the vast portion of their days are spent sitting and getting very little exercise. (This does not mean, however, that the hens should go from a rich diet during laying to a Spartan diet of plain canary and rape as soon as they are set on their eggs.) Some breeders feel that the diet has to be plain to prevent the hen from leaving her nest too frequently, but my hens continue to receive greens and other vegetables as well as their normal seed diet while on the nest without any problems.

Overfeeding rich foods like eggfood can make a hen put on weight while on the nest, but in my experience hens tend to be very focused on sitting and leave the nest only occasionally when they are on their own. They eat very quickly and then hop back on the nest. The real problem is with the males left in the cage- males can become very obese eating eggfood with no chicks to feed and if he feeds the hen she ends up full of eggfood too- much fuller than if she had been left alone. It is best to avoid feeding eggfood often to sitting hens as they really do not need it until they have chicks to feed.

If eggfood has not been used during the conditioning period, provide a small taste of eggfood to the expectant parents a few days before chicks are due to hatch so they may become accustomed to it.

Hatching

  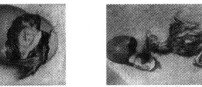

Pipping Begins   Chick Begins to Emerge   Chick and Shell

Hatching Process As Seen in A Chicken Egg

Eggs usually hatch on the 13th day but sometimes will not hatch until later depending on how tightly the hen sits. Do not discard the eggs until the 18th day at least. A breeder once threw eggs away which had not hatched on the 17th day and returned to the birdroom sometime later to hear peeping sounds coming from the garbage can- the chicks had hatched!

Eggs which are fertile and appear to be filled (meaning the chick did not die in the shell early in development) can be checked by conducting a bob test- floating them in a dish of warm water. The movements of live chicks cause the eggs to seem to bob in the water. This test is not foolproof- a breeder of my acquaintance once waited 15 days and then bobbed an egg. Detecting no motion, he cut the egg open to see at what stage of development the chick had died only to discover that the baby was in fact alive!

Some breeders look for egg shells as a sign of hatching, but hens frequently eat shells from hatched chicks. Others will hide them in seed cups or under the floor papers. I have several hens who routinely tuck all of the shells outside the cage between the wall and the breeding cage as though they know I would find them anywhere else!

Reasons for Poor Hatching
• Infertile eggs.
• Eggs too old when set.
• Improper care of eggs prior to incubation.
• Improper turning of eggs during storage.
• Weakness or illness in parent stock.
• Nutritional deficiencies in diet fed to parent stock.
• Contamination of shell.
• Cracks in shell caused by sharp toenails or accident.
• Temperatures too variable during incubation.
• Low humidity.

Chicks

Newly hatched canaries do not resemble in any way the adorable fluffy chicks most people have in mind when they think of a chick. For several days these little jellybean-sized creatures are featherless except for a bit of white fluff on the tops of their heads and backs and their eyes are tightly closed. In a 1994 *New York Times* article on canary chicks, they were noted as "look(ing) less avian than larval" and this is certainly an apt description.

Babies will often have different colored skin- clear birds will have pink skin while dark birds will have skin which is black. It often takes a day or two for skin pigmentation to develop; lightly variegated and ticked birds will usually develop pigmentation later than more heavily variegated birds.

Newly hatched chicks do not need to be fed for the first twelve hours. Chicks have some food reserves which they can draw on during this period. Hens who feed right away generally produce stronger chicks initially, but later fed chicks will catch up. All hens should begin feeding by the following morning, however.

You can determine whether chicks are being fed and are untroubled by mites in the nest by looking at their mouths when they gape for food. The inside of a well-nourished chick's mouth should be red and moist. If the lining of the mouth is pale and dry, then the chick is anemic from mites feeding on it or it is not being fed enough.

By the second day after hatching, healthy young chicks should be lively and raise their heads up to beg for food when the nest is touched. If they are lying listless in a heap at the bottom of the nest, the breeder has cause for concern.

After hatching, be sure to monitor the breeding cages frequently for chicks which have fallen or been tossed from the nest. Some cold chicks which appear nearly dead can be warmed in the hand and "returned to life," but others cannot. I have also had success with tucking cold babies beneath their warm siblings- babies seem to warm up more quickly in the nest than in the hand. Chilling usually results in some stunting of chick growth, although the chicks do catch up to their nest mates eventually. It should be noted that while chick tossing is usually caused by accident or by the hen mistaking a leg band on a chick for debris in need of removal from the nest, it can also be a sign that something is wrong with the chick.

Chicks' eyes will open on the seventh day after hatching. The eyelids open gradually and for a day or so the chicks peer out through slitted lids. Once the eyes have begun to open, the chicks imprint on their parents- if the chicks' parents are both dark birds, the chicks may not accept food from a clear bird and vice versa. Any introduction of feeder males should be done prior to this time.

If banding chicks with closed leg bands, banding usually occurs between five and seven days depending on the chick's size. Once in a while one chick in the nest will be much larger than the others and will need to be banded sooner- keep a close eye on the chicks or you may end up with a chick who is too large to band. Although most books indicate that banding should occur at seven days of age, I have banded some chicks at five days old and others at eight days. One of the best ways to tell if chicks are ready to band is to look at the development of the flight feathers on their wings- when the pinfeathers are pretty well grown out but the feathers have not yet opened, chances are good that the feet will be large enough to hold a band on the chick's leg. Banding a chick too soon just results in slipped bands.

When banding chicks, often the band seems a little tight. Sometimes books suggest using petroleum jelly or something similarly greasy to lubricate the chick's foot. Unscented talc works just as well without the mess.

Many breeders replace the nest the hen built with a new one when the babies are banded. I usually wait until the day after so I can make sure no bands have been slipped.

Once the chicks have hatched, the hen will keep the nest clean of excreta by eating the chick's droppings- this is normal and not a cause for concern. When the chicks become large enough to deposit their waste on the sides of the nest, the hen will cease to do so.

Chicks fledge- leave the nest- at about 18 days, although 21 days or more is not unheard of. A few adventurous chicks will fledge earlier while others are "nest bodies" and stay longer. Some chicks fall out of the nest for one reason or another and will remain in the nest if replaced, but once a chick is ready to fly it will just pop right back out when placed back in the nest.

Chicks instinctively take to the perches, where the parents will continue to feed them. For a few days the chicks will return to the nest to rest for short periods, so do not remove the nest right away. Within a couple of days they are flying quite well from perch to perch and between the cage floor and the perch.

Parents become very anxious when chicks first leave the nest- some look like nervous wrecks! Giving them some space by not hovering over the cage can make the transition easier for them.

Weaning Chicks

Most breeding resources indicate that chicks should be weaned at around 28 days, but this is rarely practical for first clutch babies as their mother becomes focused on her next round. Babies from the last clutch can generally be given more time, but in my experience babies begin weaning between 21 and 25 days. This is of course largely dependent on the development of the chicks. The longer they remain with the parents the better, but if they are pecking at food and being harassed by the parents they can be separated. If the chicks are being plucked, but are not ready to wean they may be placed in a cage which is hung on the side of the breeding cage and the parents will continue to feed them through the cage bars.

Fathers will generally feed chicks longer than hens will. In my experience, usually the chicks fed the longest turn out to be hens. When chicks begin eating on their own breeders should watch feeding males carefully as they may attack young males.

After chicks have been seen eating for a couple of days they can be removed to the weaning cage. No dramatic change to the diet should be made when chicks are placed in the weaning cage; only foods they have been reared on should be provided. Do not crowd weaning chicks- no more than four or five chicks to a double breeding cage. Perches should be placed as low as possible in the weaning cage- as chicks become more independent the perches can gradually be moved higher. Food in the weaning cage should be placed on the floor in shallow dishes- chicks will walk through the food and peck at it when it sticks to their feet. Small glass ashtrays and glazed plant saucers are good feeding dishes as they are heavy and flat.

Some chicks able to manage on their own in the breeding cage can regress when placed in the weaning cage so they must be monitored carefully. Chicks refusing to leave the perches to eat can be restricted to a single perch placed as close to the floor as possible.

Chicks being weaned which peep continuously are starving and should be attended. They can be placed back in with the father or the father may be placed in the weaning cage for some time.

Placing an older bird with an easy-going disposition in the cage with chicks being weaned can help teach the young birds to eat on their own by allowing them to mimic feeding behaviors.

Good first foods are well-cooked carrots- the bright orange color attracts the chicks and it is easy to eat. Other foods should include soft foods such as eggfood or nestling food, shredded wheat moistened with carrot or apple juice, cooked couscous, soak seed, and greens. Some small pellets for finches and canaries should be offered as well as they will be able to eat these before they can crack seed. Some breeders scatter rolled oats directly on the clean cage floor; chicks seem to notice it and peck at it.

Chicks will not be able to crack seed for at least six weeks and probably will not be able to fully support themselves on seed until a few weeks later. During this time they must have access at all times to foods they can eat. The introduction of unlimited quantities of hard seed too early can result in the loss of chicks- don't rush them onto hard seed too quickly. I introduce small amounts of seed at five weeks or so but continue providing soft foods right up until chicks begin the baby molt.

Chicks in the weaning cage tend to become fascinated by each other's tail feathers. Providing young birds with plenty of toys will help alleviate this. Chicks which continue plucking their cage mates must be separated. Placing them with other aggressive pluckers usually solves the problem as pluckers will generally not allow themselves to be plucked.

Some breeders insist that chicks cannot receive a bath until they are six weeks old out of concern that they will inhale water and develop chronic respiratory problems, but I routinely allow birds to bathe from the start and have not seen any problems arise from doing so.

Chicks can easily be lost during the weaning period due to illness. Careful husbandry can largely prevent such losses. Diligent attention to ensuring that cage papers and perches are clean and that all scattered eggfood is removed from the cage is vital. Take care to not become absorbed in the tending of second clutches to the detriment of first clutch chicks.

Young Birds
Young male American Singer canaries may begin to sing in the breeding cage, but more

commonly begin by the age of five weeks. A few males will lurk with the hens for a while, but generally all males will sing by the age of six months.

Young hens may sing a little. Especially around the age of six to eight months, hens twitter quite a bit and can be mistaken for males. Their song tends to be quieter, softer, and shorter than that of a male however.

Most breeders wait until babies are six to eight weeks old to transfer babies to the walk-in flight. I breed in tabletop flights and not in the smaller breeding cages which are more commonly used so my young birds are accustomed to flight from the time they leave the nest. I generally give young birds a week in the weaning cage and if they are eating well they go into the walk-in flight at about four to five weeks. This rapid transition is not common practice, but I have done it for four years and not lost a single young bird because of it. Everyone in the large flight receives the same diet of daily soft food and vegetables, pellets and seed.

Feeder Males and Foster Hens

The wise breeder never sells an excellent feeder male as they are invaluable in the breeding room. A male which has an amiable personality, doesn't pester a sitting hen, and is also willing to feed the chicks of a hen he has not mated with is worth his weight in gold!

Males often feed better than hens, which frequently become distracted by the call of a new nest before her chicks are on their own. Once the chicks have enough feathers to keep themselves warm the male can take over their care entirely if the hen is insistent on going to nest again, begins plucking the babies, looks unwell, etc.

Feeder males should be placed in the breeding cage as soon as possible- my best feeder male is always placed in with the hen after she has been set on her full clutch. After a few days he will begin to feed the hen and even stand in the nest when the hen gets off to eat. This male has not mated in the past three years, but he has raised lots of babies!

Hens that never produce fertile eggs, come from inferior stock, or are past their peak productive period can still prove useful if they build nests and feed well. Setting up one or two of these hens is an excellent insurance policy should anything go wrong with more valuable hens.

Fostering chicks who have feathered is not usually successful. Once in a while a chick that is the same color as the other chicks in a nest can be placed in a nest of other chicks of the same size just before the lights go out and it will be accepted by the foster parents. Very often though, the chick is rejected.

Problems with Hens

If hens that build nests and sit normally but refuse to lay are given fertile eggs, often the process of raising babies will jump-start the hen into laying eggs of her own.

Experienced hens and males are less likely to cause trouble in the breeding cage as they seem to be calmer and to have learned from past experience. An older male can be an asset to a first-time mother, sometimes forcing her off the nest to feed cheeping chicks.

Some young hens who abandon their first nest when the eggs begin to hatch are fine with their second clutch. The best mother I currently have in my birdroom became completely spooked when the very first egg hatched beneath her and all the eggs had to be fostered. With her second nest- and every one since- she has been a model mother.

Hens should be as close as possible to a year old before breeding. The younger the hen, the more likely problems will occur during the breeding season.

Overbreeding seriously compromises a hen's constitution. Frequently a hen allowed too many nests will be found dead atop the nest or, should she survive the breeding season, die during the molt. Offspring of overbred hens tend to less healthy and of lower quality as well.

The true strain of breeding is feeding the babies- the more babies fed, the larger the demands on the body's reserves. As long as their nutritional needs are met, hens can safely lay many more eggs than they can raise babies. The best way to get lots of babies from a valuable hen is to allow her to nest and raise babies once, then build a second nest and lay another clutch. Remove all the eggs she lays in the second round and foster them under another hen. Recycle the hen by releasing her back into the hen flight for a couple of weeks and then allow her go to nest for a third time and raise the babies. Again allow her another nest, foster the eggs, and then release her back into the hen flight for a well-deserved rest! In this way you can get four nests of babies from the hen without straining her.

When determining whether or not to allow a hen a second nest consider the health of the hen before anything else- certainly before her level of eagerness to go to nest again. Many hens will happily breed themselves to exhaustion- it is poor management to allow her to do so.

Some hens have a mind of their own when it comes to placement of the nest and despite the efforts of the breeder will persist in laying eggs in a seed cup. It is generally easiest to give into the hen in this matter and simply remove the seed cup and place a plastic nesting cup there. Usually the hen will be thrilled with this alteration and build her nest there. (Providing food in dishes on the floor of the cage discourages fixation on seed cups as nest sites.)

Once in a while a hen will insist on a truly odd placement but as long as it is not completely unworkable she should be humored. Many breeders have a particular place for the nest and hens either build in it or not at all, but in a season when so many complications can arise I chose to pick my battles with hens carefully and allow them their individual eccentricities as much as possible. The only really strange place I've ever had a canary hen nest was in the dish on the floor of the cage where I place clean nesting material to be used in building a nest. A young hen, she apparently considered the carrying of material up from the dish to the plastic nesting cup a waste of time and used the nest provided . . . She laid her eggs in the dish, hatched and fed the chicks there, and they fledged perfectly. When she went to nest for a second time, she chose to use a plastic nest cup instead of the dish of material on the floor.

I also offer my hens a selection of nest placements, placing two or three plastic nests in the cage and removing the extras after the hen has chosen her nest. Hens who prefer the same location for their second nest can be allowed this by placing the first nest with babies on the other side of the cage- she will continue to feed them- and placing a new nest in the original location. Trying to convince the hen to accept a different location usually results in eggs being laid in the old nest, where they are trampled and fouled by the hen's babies from the first nest.

Hens who seem to have digestive upsets from eating the droppings of the chicks can be treated with a pinch or two of Epsom salt in the drinking water. Some breeders have also used this treatment for hens that refuse to feed as it produces a laxative effect, forcing the hen to leave the nest to relieve herself. The stimulation of the sight of hungry chicks begging for food when she returns will hopefully induce the hen to feed.

Hens that absolutely refuse to leave the nest may be forced to do so by removing the nest from the cage for a short period of time and providing something tasty and nutritious for her to eat. While the nest is gone she will eat the food and when the nest is returned she should feed the chicks. Some breeders feel that the nest should be removed from the hen's sight, but I have had luck simply hanging it on the outside of the cage.

Don't assume that the hen is not feeding if you do not catch sight of her doing so. Some hens are stealthy and feed only when no one is looking. Hens also have different feeding habits- some will feed small amounts often, while others feed large amounts less often. Both work just fine. If the chicks have food in their crops and seem to be growing, then the hen is feeding.

When it comes to hens, the one truth is that they are all individuals and respond to change differently. Some hens are better feeders when left alone to raise their chicks while some depend on the presence of a mate to feed her and help feed the babies. A hen who is a wonderful mother when left alone may become a terrible one when a mate is left with her and one who is great when helped by a male may be unable to manage by herself. Other hens are pretty adaptable.

Sometimes a hen refuses to feed and a male would be perfectly able and willing to feed the chicks but the hen refuses to budge from the nest. If the chicks are not growing well and are not being fed properly, action of some sort must be taken. Very young chicks can be fostered to other nests if they are available. The hen might also be removed to another cage several times a day for a short period of time to allow the male to feed and then placed back in the cage to keep the babies warm. If the chicks have developed feathers and can keep themselves warm, removing the hen from the cage and leaving the male to care for the young may be the best action as moving feathered chicks to foster nests is usually unsuccessful.

A hen who abandons her chicks can sometimes be encouraged to tend to the babies by removing all the perches in the cage and forcing her to perch on the edge of the nest.

Once the chicks have begun feathering out the hen will spend less and less time on the nest. If there are several chicks in a nest they will produce quite a bit of body heat, more than enough to keep themselves warm once they have some feathering.

Hens that sleep frequently on the nest while sitting on eggs are likely sick or getting close to the molt. Watch her closely as she will probably not raise her young. Fostering the eggs is preferable to leaving them under a hen like this. Hens who feed poorly that have previously been good mothers may also be ill or nearing the molt.

Hens that pluck their chicks to build a new nest should be given some lengths of twine or cotton string tied to the cage bars to tug at, pieces of soft white unscented toilet paper, and other things which will distract her from pulling at her babies' feathers. Should the hen continue, a product called Bitter Apple spray can be applied to the chicks' feathers with a cotton swab. Usually Bitter Apple works well to dissuade a hen from plucking. Rarely a hen will pluck her chicks bloody, mutilating them. Leaving chicks with this sort of mother is dangerous- either they or the mother must be pulled immediately. If the chicks are feathered out enough to keep themselves warm and a feeder male is in the cage, remove the hen and allow him to feed. If no male is available, the nest should be placed in a nursery cage hung on the side of the breeding cage so that the mother can feed through the bars but cannot reach her babies' feathers.

Vicious feather pluckers should never be given a second chance. There is no permanent remedy for this behavior. If the hen is valuable she may be used in the future for egg production but all eggs should be fostered. Egg eaters are usually incurable, but make sure that the hen is truly an egg destroyer and not merely cleaning up an egg which has been broken in the nest through some accident. Feather pluckers and egg eaters should not be passed along to other breeders- this is unscrupulous at best!

Problems in the Breeding Room
Large problems in the breeding room can be caused by very small things. An experienced

breeder once began to lose entire nests of young chicks with no obvious cause- the parents seemed to be in excellent health and the affected nests were scattered through the breeding room. Sometimes the dead babies had full crops while at other times they had empty crops despite the fact that all parents seemed to be feeding . . . The cause was discovered through sheer chance when the breeder happened to be in the room the moment the lights came on in the morning and discovered a hen with a nest of chicks hurriedly scrambling to her nest from a perch. After investigating, the breeder discovered  the nest of chicks cold and lifeless. Apparently the nightlight used in the birdroom had burned out and hens were unable to return to their nests after the lights went out! After the bulb in the nightlight was replaced, the problem was completely resolved.

Some breeders use a string of Christmas lights in the breeding room at night for very low intensity light at night. Alternatively, one can conduct a "hen check" every night as soon as the lights turn off- use a flashlight and check to make sure that each hen is back on her nest. Hens which have been caught off the nest seem very grateful for the assistance and scramble back to their nests quickly.

Mice and loud noises can also startle hens off the nest at night.

Some males are meddlesome in the breeding cage- tearing apart nests, insisting on breeding with sitting hens, refusing to allow the hen off the nest, or even eating eggs. The first issue is most common in young males who seem to be so excited by the nest building process that they don't want it to end. These males generally improve with experience. The second type of problem male is more of a nuisance than anything- they are responding to their own increased hormone levels and the breeding activity going on throughout the room. Hens, unless unusually timid, will usually set these oversexed males straight without intervention from the breeder. The third type of male takes his role too seriously and insists that the hen remain on the nest at all times- chasing her about the cage should she leave to eat, drink, or relieve herself. Unless the hen becomes overly distressed or serious fighting occurs between the two they will generally sort the situation out for themselves. The egg eater is a bird of a different color- he poses a very real threat to the nest. Males which have developed this habit but are valuable may be used as studs. They must be removed from the breeding cage at night and cannot be returned the next morning until the hen has laid and the egg has been pulled and replaced with a plastic egg. Once the hen has been set on her eggs, the male should not be placed in the cage again as some will actually chase a setting hen off the nest to get at the eggs. Even if this does not happen the eggs are at risk every time the hen leaves the nest.

It should be noted, however, that egg eating birds are actually rare. Perfectly innocent males who simply clean up an egg which fell out of the nest can be mislabeled as egg eaters. Mice have also been known to be the culprits in disappearing egg cases.

Ending the Breeding Season

One should not feel guilty cutting the breeding season off early when a manageable number of chicks have been reached.

Ending the breeding season can be challenging as some birds will insist on continuing much longer than is good for them. It does not harm the hens to lay clear eggs- the burden is in the incubation of eggs and the rearing of chicks. All eggs, however, should be removed from the flight cage as soon as possible to prevent birds from acquiring a taste for fresh eggs.

Many breeders restrict hens who continue to lay to lean rations feeling that eggfood encourages egg laying, but the hens are in need of increased nutrition during the post breeding period. The amount of eggfood provided should be reduced but not removed from the diet completely. Birds need to rebuild their reserves so that they can complete the upcoming molt healthy and strong.

My hens are generally pretty tired by the end of April when I am wrapping up breeding for the year. There are always a couple of hens who hate to see the season end and lay right up until the lights are dropped in May, but I have found that keeping the hens in a dimmer environment helps in reducing their level of interest in breeding. In my bird room I can accomplish this by simply reducing the number of light bulbs used in each fixture and covering the sides of the hen flight with sheets.

Continuing breeding into the hot summer months is asking for trouble for a multitude of reasons- soft food spoils more quickly, breeders begin molting, etc.

Chick Development- General Guidelines	
Hatching	13 days at the earliest, often later
Feathers Begin to Appear	4-5 days
Banding With Closed Bands	5-7 days depending on chick growth
Eyes Open	7 days
Feather Quills Well Developed	10-12 days old
Fledge (Leave the Nest)	18 days
Wean	23-25 days
Baby Molt	8 to 10 weeks

These dates are approximate- some chicks leave the nest several days earlier or later, for example. Weaning is generally earlier for first clutch chicks than for second clutch ones.

Quick Tips - Things I Have Learned About Breeding Canaries

- Canaries, like people, are individuals with their own personalities and preferences. There is no "one size fits all" truth about breeding canaries; though a few general guidelines are helpful, canaries can always manage to surprise even an experienced breeder. Be prepared for the unexpected and adapt to the needs of your birds.
- There is no substitute for careful husbandry. Paying close attention to what is going on in the birdroom can prevent small problems from becoming large ones.
- Relax. Birds have been managing to breed for thousands of years. Becoming stressed out over the bird's failure to proceed according to the breeder's plans will not make the birds breed any better. The birds will generally get things sorted out satisfactorily if left to their own devices. I once read in a vintage breeding book that a bottle of whiskey was a helpful supply to have on hand in the birdroom during breeding season- not for the birds, but for the breeder!
- When problems arise- and if you breed birds long enough, they *will* arise- don't panic.
- Contrary to conventional wisdom, you don't have to tiptoe around your birds. Maintain your usual routine during breeding season. If you clean the floor of the bird room every day with a shop vacuum, go ahead and do so during the breeding season. Bump the cages a little, watch television, or listen to the radio . . . As long as the birds are accustomed to the routine, they will be fine.
- Always have a backup plan. First time hens who sat beautifully may become startled when the eggs begin to hatch and refuse to cover the babies, hens die during incubation, hens quit feeding . . . Hope for the best, but prepare for the worst- try to set as many of your hens on eggs on the same day so you'll have alternative nests in which to place babies and always have a good foster hen ready.
- Have a container of a commercial hand feeding formula on hand just in case all your backups fail and you have to hand feed. The commercial food is nutritious and easy to use. Why add the extra work of making a homemade hand feeding formula to all the other work of breeding season? Store the formula in the freezer to maintain freshness, but allow it to warm to room temperature before mixing it.
- Should the worst happen and a nest of unfeathered babies is left motherless with no foster hen available, a makeshift brooder can be made by placing a five gallon glass fish tank over a heating pad, lining the tank with paper toweling, and covering the tank with a towel. Place the nest inside the tank on top of a roll of masking tape or something similar to keep the nest from tipping. Turn the heating pad on low (be sure to carefully monitor the temperature to ensure that the chicks do not become chilled or overheat). Babies can then be handfed.
- "Feeder" males are worth their weight in gold and have saved many a nest of babies- if

a male feeds like a champion but bombs at the shows, keep him anyway. He just might save a future champion!

- Don't rush your birds- most problems occur because the breeder tries to push birds which aren't ready for one reason or another into breeding. Birds allowed to come into condition naturally will produce fewer clear eggs and will sit and feed better. You may start later than you wanted to, but you'll end up at the same place in the end- and with fewer headaches.
- Don't breed poor breeders or poor feeders regardless of what they do at the shows or you can end up with a roomful of birds that all have these negative traits. I personally never breed a flaky hen (one who startles off the nest easily, sits too tight or not enough, etc.) more than twice- every hen gets a second chance, but if they are still giving you problems after the second nest they'll do it every time. Hens that make the breeder stand on his or her head to make sure everything comes out okay aren't worth the effort.
- Develop and maintain a network of "breeder buddies"- these folks can provide advice and much needed support.
- Keep notes on your birds throughout the year, including pairings you would like to make. With all the work and general busyness of getting the birdroom situated and birds set up, often one will forget exactly what one had planned or find oneself wondering why one wanted a certain pairing. Good, complete records are invaluable!
- Hens can be wild cards in breeding. Hens carry the song of their fathers; while their brothers may have similar songs, listening to the father is preferable. The hen's call notes can sometimes indicate what they carry, but are much less reliable than hearing the father.
- Don't sell hens too quickly- too many novices buy hens, try them out for a year, and then sell them before they can make a proper determination about what the hens are carrying.
- Sometimes a different pairing will produce better offspring. If a hen comes from good quality stock, give her at least two seasons with different mates before deciding to sell her. Breeding her sons and grandsons back to her may be the best way to achieve stock of her caliber.
- Many experienced breeders believe that the best way to introduce a particular "sound" into one's stock is to bring in a hen carrying the song you'd like to have- using a male is much less effective.
- Using a tutor will teach the birds new notes, but it will not be a part of the birds' genetic song- if one wants a sound to remain, it needs to be bred into the birds.
- Purchase new breeding stock well in advance of the start of breeding season to allow the birds to become adjusted to their new environment.
- Be aware that if breeding stock is purchased from a breeder who has a very different breeding schedule from that of your own (he begins in March, but you would like to begin in January), the birds are going to have difficulty adjusting the first breeding season. Sometimes no matter what one does, the birds will simply not come into proper

condition until later into the breeding season. In this case it is best to allow them to come into condition slowly and just set them up when one is setting up one's other birds for a second round. I have battled with hens several times in these cases and the hens will win every time!

- Do not breed more birds than you can handle. Many novices breed large numbers of birds, especially when they have not won at the shows- after all, more birds mean more chances to win! The trick is to know when to stop- in the excitement of breeding season it is easy to lose sight of the fact that a lot of birds means a lot of work for many, many months. The experienced breeder knows how many birds he can handle and resists the temptation to breed more than that quantity.

Breeding-Related Health Issues

Things Which Can Affect Fertility in Both Males and Hens

- Excess salt has been noted as reducing fertility and hatchability of eggs in poultry and depresses growth in young birds. There has been some suggestion that salt can also cause fertility problems in male birds as well.
- Mite infestations can decrease fertility in males, egg production in hens, and weight gain in young chicks.
- Often nutritional deficiencies do not become obvious until breeding season. For this reason attention to proper nutrition is vital year-round, not just in the weeks prior to and during breeding season.
- Sometimes new breeding stock fails to produce well the first year due to being introduced to a new management system or prior nutritional deficiencies. Very often these birds will do quite well the following breeding season given the chance.

Hens and Eggs

- Soft-shelled eggs are most often caused by calcium deficiency. Certain foods can reduce the absorption of calcium so that even hens receiving adequate dietary calcium produce soft-shelled eggs. These foods include those with high levels of oxalic acid, which binds calcium and other nutrients needed by breeding birds. Vegetables high in oxalic acid are: spinach, chard, beets and beet leaves, purslane, parsley, chives, cassava, and amaranth. These vegetables are okay in small quantities, but should be excluded from the diet during breeding.
- Another thing that can cause soft-shelled eggs is producing eggs too closely together; the eggs bump up against each other in the shell gland. An odd soft-shelled egg produced in a hen which lays hard-shelled eggs both before and after is probably caused by this. There is some suggestion in poultry literature that it can also be caused by hens being disturbed by unusual noise or activity.
- The common wisdom is that unusually small or large eggs are sterile, but as with many other aspects of canary breeding surprises can happen so do not discard these eggs.
- Abnormally large or thick shelled eggs can be caused by cold or damp conditions or by poor diet. These eggs can be difficult to pass and may lead to egg binding or prolapse of the oviduct. Should the egg be laid, the thickness of the egg can cause the chick to be unable to hatch.
- Overbreeding and internal damage to the reproductive organs of a hen can also result in defective eggs.
- On occasion, an egg may be found that has blood on it. This is usually not serious and affects only a few eggs of a clutch. Sometimes the addition of a small amount of oily

seed such as flax seed can help a hen that occasionally bleeds when passing eggs. A hen which does so frequently may have an infection in her oviduct.

- Maintaining proper humidity- at least 40% for canaries- is important as low humidity is a common cause of eggs failing to hatch. This humidity level can be achieved through the use of a humidifier or by lightly misting the eggs with water. Allowing the hen to bathe every day for a couple of days before eggs are due to hatch is thought to help as well.

- Hens which build nests and sit but fail to lay may be ovulating normally, but rather than proceeding normally through the reproductive system, the yolk is dropping into the abdominal cavity. This can happen due to obstruction in the oviduct following infection.

- Other causes of hens becoming stalled in the breeding process include stress, dietary restriction, and other environmental problems.

- Sudden deaths of laying hens may be caused by deficiencies in calcium, potassium, phosphorus, or Vitamin D.

- Once in a while a canary which does not sing and never comes into breeding condition may be found. They are almost universally considered hens. However, in certain rare instances this bird may be found to be genderless in that it has underdeveloped sex organs or may even possess the gonads of both sexes. Sex reversal in other species of birds has also been witnessed, primarily in hens which gradually develop male sex organs following damage to an ovary. Instances have been reported in which such a (former) hen has fertilized another hen. This information is provided so that the reader may be aware that failure to breed on a hen's part can be complicated by issues at which the breeder cannot even begin to guess.

Males

- The testes of male birds do not become fully functional until they are in full breeding condition. Attempting to rush the breeding season by putting birds together before they are completely ready results in a high percentage of clear, unfertilized eggs. Male birds will mate readily before they are in peak breeding condition, but they produce lower quantities of sperm which are less active than those produced when males are in condition.

- Hens are frequently blamed for fertility problems, but males can be just as much to blame. The only way to test a male's fertility is to mate him with a number of different hens. Male infertility can be caused by lack of breeding condition and physical problems such as tumors, reproductive tract infection, anatomical defects, etc. Additionally, nutritional deficiencies and obesity can also cause fertility problems.

- Another more controversial cause of lowered fertility is excessive or careless line breeding. Line breeding can be done for many generations so long as very careful attention is paid to the health of the individual birds being bred and only those birds in the best of health are bred as any health defect present in a line of birds may be intensified by line breeding. A number of top breeders in the American Singer fancy line breed and experience no problems as a result but there have been cases where heavily line bred birds have shown reduced vigor and strength resulting in lowered fertility and even sterility followed by atypically short life spans. Whether or not this is the result of line breeding in and of itself or of incorrect line breeding I cannot say. I only provide the observation to stress the need for proceeding with great care and diligent attention when line breeding.

Clear and Addled Eggs, Dead in Shell Chicks

- When an egg appears dark but is filled with a thick, foul-smelling substance, it has become addled. Improper handling on the part of the breeder or a mishap of some sort in the nest can cause this. These eggs should be removed from the nest as soon as they are discovered to prevent their breaking and the contents fouling the nest.
- An often overlooked cause of dead in shell babies and weak nestlings is infection in the hen's reproductive tract. Some breeders administer a course of antibiotics prior to breeding to prevent this.
- Some chicks die in the shell due to being abnormally positioned- the head being at the small end of the egg, for example.
- Another cause of dead, unhatched chicks is chilling of the eggs through not being properly covered by a hen who is inexperienced, thin in the breast, or who has too large a clutch. Sometimes hens get caught off the nest and the eggs chill overnight.
- Eggshells which are chipped or cracked will cause chicks to die. Keeping the hen's nails clipped will prevent her from accidentally chipping the shells with sharp toenails when she turns the eggs in the nest.

Health Emergencies during Breeding Season

- Egg binding is a condition in which a hen is unable to pass a fully formed egg due to the size of the egg, hypocalcaemia, or lack of condition. Other things which may cause egg binding include hens being too young or too old, overbreeding, malformation of the egg, or inflammation or obstructions within the oviduct.
- I can also attest from personal experience that introducing strange males into the aviary can sometimes induce hens to begin laying when they are out of condition and lead to egg binding.
- Egg binding is a serious emergency because it frequently leads to death and is always fatal if left untreated. Hens may begin to appear rather dull and poorly the evening before an egg is to be laid but often the first signs that something is wrong occur late in the morning, when the hen begins to appear to be in distress. She may sit in the nest, on a perch, or on the cage floor with feathers puffed up, breathing heavily with her beak open, straining to pass the egg. Immediate treatment is necessary. One of the most effective ways to treat an egg bound hen is to take a dish of hot water, cover the dish with plastic wrap and then cover the plastic wrap with a towel. After testing the heat with the inside of one's wrist to ensure that it is not too hot, place the hen on the towel

and cover her with a cloth to prevent her flying away once she begins to feel better. Allow the warmth to penetrate the inflamed tissues and cause the tissues to relax. Often the hen will be able to pass the egg with this treatment alone. A drop of warm olive oil can be dropped on the cloaca - the reasoning being that the oil will lubricate the passage of the egg.

- Sometimes exercise is helpful so if the egg bound hen appears to feel better after the warmth treatment but has not yet passed the egg, placing her in a tabletop flight will often help her to do so.

- The single most important preventive treatment for egg binding is year-round access to free flight such as that which is permitted in a floor to ceiling aviary. This provides the necessary exercise to develop the strength in the abdominal muscles needed to pass an egg. Other things thought to prevent egg binding include feeding nyger and flaxseed, allowing free access to cuttlebone, and scraping cuttlebone onto food if a hen refuses to use the cuttlebone. Avoid breeding hens younger than a year old and restrict the number of clutches a hen is permitted to produce. Obesity can also lead to this problem.

- Prolapse of the oviduct- a condition in which the oviduct protrudes outside of the cloaca- can occur when a hen is laying. Causes include severe or longstanding bowel infections and other problems such as tumors, cysts, ruptures, and the delayed passing of eggs which result in increased pressure within the abdomen. Treatment of this condition by anyone other than a veterinarian is almost always ineffective and fatal. Successful treatment involves surgically fixing the oviduct within the abdominal cavity. Fortunately, it is rare and can best be avoided by breeding only hens in excellent health and treating all cases of egg binding without delay.

- Normally an egg is released directly into the oviduct and laid. Sometimes, however, an egg can be released into the abdominal cavity where it can lead to peritonitis. Symptoms include all those of any generalized illness- listlessness, lethargy, etc. The abdomen may appear distended and respiratory distress may also be evident. This condition is almost always fatal even with veterinary care, but should the hen recover recurrence is likely.

- Sometimes a chick will develop a black spot on its abdomen which is unrelated to skin pigmentation. The cause could be bleeding from the intestines or other organs- whatever the cause, this condition is nearly always fatal. There has been some speculation that at least in some cases the bleeding is caused by a bowel infection.

Chart of Color Pairings

	Yellow Male	White Male	Blue Male	Green Male
Yellow Hen	100% Yellow	50% Yellow 50% White	50% Yellow Variegated 50% White Variegated	100% Yellow Variegated
White Hen	50% Yellow 50% White	50% White 25% Yellow 25% Non-viable due to lethal factor	50% White Variegated 25% Yellow Variegated 25% Non-viable due to lethal factor	50% Yellow Variegated 50% White Variegated
Blue Hen	50% Yellow Variegated 50% White Variegated	50% White Variegated 25% Yellow Variegated 25% Non-viable due to lethal factor	50% Blue 25% White Variegated 25% Non-viable due to lethal factor	50% Blue 50% Green
Green Hen	100% Yellow Variegated	50% Yellow Variegated 50% White Variegated	50% Blue 50% Green	100% Greens and Yellow Variegated

This chart refers only to color, not to feather type and presumes that the heredity of the birds in question is pure- for example, that both yellow birds possess only genes for yellow. It is entirely possible for two yellow birds to throw variegated chicks or for heavily variegated birds to throw clear yellows due to genes inherited from their parents or grandparents.

It is important to remember that the statistical percentage listed is for each chick- not for the entire nest. It's an entirely new roll of the dice for each bird. In a nest of four chicks from a yellow and white pairing one will not necessarily end up with a 50/50 split but any possible combination.

Yellow, green and cinnamon birds are yellow ground color birds while white and blue are white ground birds. Breeding two dominant white birds together will cause the lethal factor to be expressed- approximately 25% of chicks will die in the shell early in development.

Cinnamon Inheritance

Cinnamon factor is a complicated issue due to its nature as a sex-linked, recessive characteristic. It can remain hidden for many generations and pop up in unexpected places.

Cinnamon is characterized by brown feathering due to the absence of the color black in the feathers. Cinnamons can range from lightly variegated through completely cinnamon (a cinnamon self). A clear bird may be cinnamon genetically, but if it lacks melanin (variegation) it will not show it. Clear cinnamon birds reportedly give away their true genetic color by producing a gleam of red in the eye in bright light.

Chicks which have red eyes should be noted- the eyes will darken after they open. Should the red-eyed chick feather out any color other than cinnamon, it is a cinnamon carrier. Cinnamon chicks appearing in the nest of non cinnamon parents can be sexed as hens. Should the mother be cinnamon and the father a cinnamon carrier, cinnamon chicks may be either sex.

It should be noted that hens are what they appear to be- they cannot carry the cinnamon factor unless they <u>are</u> cinnamon. Unless, of course the hen is clear and has no variegation- in that case she would appear to be yellow, white or red depending on her ground color.

	Normal Male	Cinnamon Carrier Male	Cinnamon Male
Normal Hen	Normal Males, Normal Hens	Carrier Males, Normal Males, Cinnamon Hens, Normal Hens	Carrier Males, Cinnamon Hens
Cinnamon Hen	Carrier Males, Normal Hens	Cinnamon Males, Carrier Males, Cinnamon Hens, Normal Hens	Cinnamon Males, Cinnamon Hens

Variegation

When it comes to genetics, the unscientifically minded breeder is at a distinct disadvantage- while the introduction of a more scientific treatment of inheritance in the canary is obviously beneficial, issues like melanin production and suppression can leave the ordinary person very confused. Those who write scientifically about genetic inheritance tend to write, well, *scientifically*. As anyone who has any familiarity at all with science is aware, it has its own unique language and manner of speaking which can be difficult for non scientists.

Variegation is most simply defined as having dark feathers (or more complexly as expressing melanin or pigmentation). It is entirely separate from color. Variegated birds can be any of the three ground colors- yellow, white, or red. In his book *Colored Canaries*, G. B. R. Walker- who is a leading colorbred fancier in Britain- writes that "areas of the body most likely to possess variegation are the crown of the head, the eyes and cheek, breast, flank, wings, outer tail feathers and the back."

Classification of variegation is as follows:

> *Ticked*: dark marking smaller than a dime (two ticked marks would be considered a
>   lightly variegated bird).
> *Light Variegated*: less than 50% dark markings.
> *Medium Variegated*: between 50% and 74% dark markings.
> *Heavily Variegated*: more than 75% dark markings but less than 100%.
> *Foul*: all dark except for one or two light feathers in the wing flights or tail.
> *Self*: all dark, no light feathers at all.

Inheritance of variegation is a mystery to most novices- how can clear, variegated, and dark birds appear in the same nest? I cannot claim to be able to explain the complex genetic reasons for this but will simply address the issue most unscientifically minded breeders such as myself care about- what will be produced when two medium variegated birds are bred? That answer is as follows: chances are 25% clear or ticked, 25% self or foul, and 50% medium variegated. That said, one should be aware that these statistical probabilities are NOT for the nest, but for each individual chick's chances of coming out with a particular variegation pattern. For each and every chick, the dice is rolled anew. This is why in a nest of four chicks, one can come up with all sorts of combinations other than the 1/1/2 combination one would expect without this understanding.

Canaries can only express (or show) black and brown pigments. A number of different genes for pigmentation production or suppression are carried by all canaries- how these genes are combined determines the quantity and location of markings. Variegation is caused by a mutation which first appeared in the canary hundreds of years ago that resulted in birds different from the normal green canary in which black pigment is present all over the body. A different mutation causes the expression of only brown pigmentation, leaving only the warm brown color termed "cinnamon."

There is a common perception that closed populations of canaries will tend to darken over time but many assert the opposite to be the case- that variegation will tend to decrease, resulting in lighter birds. However, according to Judy Snider's *"Canary Colors"* article (contained in the DRAGON, ASC Chapter 22 library), "clear canaries can only be reliably produced after six generations of rigorous culling."

Interestingly, G. B. R. Walker in his book, *Colored Canaries*, states that inferior quality clear birds result from the pairing of clear to clear year after year. He states that self, foul or variegated green birds should be introduced in alternate years not only to maintain color quality but also to prevent birds from losing size.

Variegated Canary

Molting

The Molting Season

- The molt generally lasts six to eight weeks and constitutes one of the most physically demanding periods of a bird's life. Special care and attention during this period will pay dividends throughout the rest of the year.
- Birds go through two normal types of molts in their lives- the baby molt, which occurs at about eight to ten weeks of age, and an annual molt. During the baby molt, none of the longer feathers of the tail or wings are lost- thus a young bird is called an "unflighted" bird. Older birds which have molted their long feathers are called "flighted" birds.
- Abnormal molting is called a soft molt or an unseasonable molt. Molting more than one time a year is abnormal for a canary. Abnormal molts can be caused by stress, heat, drafts, changes in lighting (especially length of daytime hours), and illness.
- During the molt birds may be housed together if they are provided extra room and not crowded. Males in full molt will generally leave each other alone if placed into a third cage (one which neither male has claimed as his territory) and will cohabitate more or less peacefully until they begin to come back into song. Hens and males may also be housed together during this period as neither will be in breeding condition. As the end of the molt approaches, older males will become scrappier with their roommates and will need to be removed to separate quarters. Young males which have never been housed separately usually manage to coexist peacefully for a longer period of time but will also begin to fight as they come into full song.
- A rapid molt is better than a slow one. A bird which drags its way slowly through a molt is probably not in the best of health.
- Crowding birds together during the molt will almost always lead to them plucking each other's feathers, sometimes mercilessly. Provide birds plenty of space and watch out for aggressive (and overly passive) birds- these will need to be separated from the rest of the flock. In addition to overcrowding, things which can cause feather plucking are excessive light and nutritional imbalances.
- Sometimes even when given plenty of room, birds will feather pluck. Provide birds with lots of things to play with such as lengths of sisal twine tied to perches or the sides of the cage and other preening-type toys. One of the best toys I have found is a roll of white unscented toilet paper hung above perches in the flight at a height where birds on a perch can just reach the roll. My birds do not pluck each other at all when given rolls of toilet paper to pick at.
- Many years ago providing birds with a piece of salt pork was thought to help reduce

feather plucking. Depending on the writer, the reasoning was either that the birds craved the salt or that the salt would satisfy birds which had come to enjoy the salty taste of the blood they drew when plucking their neighbors. Some breeders today suggest giving birds salted cooked rice for this same purpose. I personally remain leery of adding too much salt to a canary's diet as their bodies are not able to handle it. I prefer to use toys and segregation of offending individuals.

- When pinfeathers begin to appear on the heads of your birds, the molt is nearly complete!
- Nearly all males quit singing during the molt. Some birds may continue to sing, but their song will be softer, shorter and less frequent.
- It is commonly believed that birds learn song best during the molt. This is an ideal time to play canary song tapes and CDs as well as classical music for the birds to study.
- Lighting is generally dimmed for the duration of the molt to allow the birds to remain calmer. Dimmer lighting also protects coloration in the new feathers, which sunlight can fade.
- The number of hours of lighting can be reduced drastically during the molt. I wait until the end of breeding season when all chicks are completely weaned and in the walk-in flight and turn the lights down to 9 to 9½ hours all at once. This causes the birds to quickly begin to molt. Some breeders go in the other direction- increasing the hours of daylight to 15 hours or more, but I was told about the short hour method when I first began breeding canaries and it has worked quite well. The birds molt very quickly and the increased nighttime hours gives them more quiet time so they are less stressed.
- Avoid any undue stress on the birds at this time- moving a molting bird can sometimes result in death due to stress! Molting season is a very poor time to buy or sell birds for this reason.
- Ensure that birds receive good nutrition throughout the molt. Increase the levels of protein, vitamins and minerals by including bee pollen, eggfood, spirulina and other supplements in their diet more frequently. Watch birds closely for evidence of gout- if their legs and feet begin to appear reddened or seem irritated, cut back on the protein level in their diet.
- A small amount of seeds which are high in oil- such as nyger or flax- should be offered twice a week during this period to promote a nice luster in the new feathers.
- Offering rolled oats of the type used by people for breakfast cereal will speed the molt along. Oats are high in carbohydrates- 30% higher than canary seed. Oats are easily digested and provide the extra energy needed by molting birds. Birds must be watched for excessive weight gain while being fed oats because they are high in calories and can

be fattening so this food is best reserved for those times when birds need extra energy-such as during the molt.

- Offer raw shredded carrots, sweet potatoes, broccoli, and other vegetables high in carotenes to promote good feather coloration. While colorbred birds must be fed artificial coloring agents during the molt to achieve their best coloration, this is not permitted in American Singers which will be exhibited.
- Certain watery foods such as cucumber are thought to trigger the molt.
- Provide cuttlebone and other sources of calcium as this is an essential element in the growth of good quality feathers.
- Allow birds to bathe regularly- every day if possible. This will help soften the sheaths on the developing feathers, ease the itchiness which seems to accompany molting, and will minimize birds picking on each other's feathers as they will be busy preening their own. Cold water from the tap will do just fine- feathers seem to have more luster when birds are allowed to bathe in cold water.
- The addition of a small amount of Listerine or cider vinegar to a bird's bathing water will assist in deterring mites and will give the feathers a nice appearance. Additionally, both Listerine and cider vinegar have mild antibacterial properties which may help to prevent some skin infections.
- Exercise during the molting period is as important as any other time in a bird's life- just as walking back and forth from the couch to the refrigerator hardly constitutes a healthy exercise program for a human being, living in a small cage which only requires hopping from perch to seed cup will negatively affect a bird's health!
- Do not try to stop a molt- once begun, the best thing to do is hasten the process.
- Failing to molt once a year is also a problem. If, despite increasing the room temperature and changing the hours of daylight to which the bird is exposed, it has not begun to molt by early fall then plucking a few tail feathers should cause a bird to molt.
- By carefully controlling all light and heat-related molting triggers in the environment of a group of canaries, scientists have been able to prevent molting. Unfortunately the scientists then discovered that failing to molt at all will cause canaries to die! Despite the inconvenience of vacuuming up feathers every day and not being able to listen to your singer's song for a few months, this is obviously a vital biological function for your birds.
- Hens who have been overworked during the breeding season often fail to survive the molt. These birds have exhausted their physical reserves and lack the physical health to make it through the molt. Should they manage to survive, their feather quality will be poorer than that of hens managed properly.
- Birds which have not received proper nutrition throughout the year will show this lack during the molt more than any other time of the year.
- Robert Stroud noted that birds whose dietary needs are not met during the molt have a way of getting even by dropping dead shortly after molting despite having appeared to

molt normally. Other birds will become what are known in breeding circles as "vampires." A vampire is a bird which never regains complete health- refusing to come into breeding condition or sing- but seems to hang on forever.

- Molting cornbread may be a better choice for feeding during the molt as it will not spoil in the warmer temperatures of the molting period.
- Breeders should note birds which have difficulties getting through the molt- these birds will generally be poor choices for one's breeding program due to their lack of good physical health.
- Old males will take longer after they have finished molting to return to full song. This is a normal result of the aging process and not a cause for concern unless the song does not return at all.

When Your Bird Molts Out of Season

I receive more phone calls about canaries that have stopped singing than for any other reason. This is one of the largest sources of concern for many as canaries are prized for their beautiful song. The most common cause for lack of singing in a healthy young bird which has previously sung freely is molting, which is often poorly understood by many pet owners.

Birds are biologically hardwired to respond to certain environmental factors by molting, which is a six to eight week process of replacing all the feathers on their bodies. Feathers become worn and tattered with constant use over time and nature has provided for this by causing birds to molt once a year- usually in the summer. This allows a bird in the wild to produce a new set of feathers to replace the old during a period of time when good food sources tend to be at their highest levels and before the hardships of the winter season begin. The first molt of a bird's life occurs at about eight to ten weeks of age and involves only the smaller feathers of the body. Birds which are a year old or older will lose all of their feathers including the longer feathers of the wings and tail.

The molting process is orderly- the feathers are lost in a predetermined pattern beginning with the upper chest area and working through different symmetrical parts of the body until reaching the top of the head. When small white pinfeathers (so named because they look like small pins- these are developing feathers which are still wrapped in a keratinous sheath) appear on the head, the molt is approaching completion. The process can take as few as six weeks or as long as ten weeks. A shorter molt is better as this period is very stressful physically for a bird. Molts which continue for longer than twelve weeks are a sign of a health or environmental problem.

A healthy pet bird kept in the proper environment will only molt one time a year. Birds which are ill will sometimes go into what is called a "soft molt" in which they will lose small feathers year round- this is an issue which should be addressed by an avian veterinarian. The most common cause of unseasonable molting, however, is exposure to one or more molting triggers- heat, draft, and increased hours of light. Small birds such as canaries are especially susceptible to changes in their environment and the conditions found in many pet homes result in unnecessary stress caused by frequent molting. Birds, unlike cats or dogs, must be kept in fairly controlled environments with a set period of lighting and protection from changes in temperature fluctuations and drafts- warm or cold.

The ideal environment for a pet canary is one in which he is exposed only to natural day length, is kept at a constant temperature of somewhere between 50-72 degrees, and in an area free of drafts.

I receive a number of phone calls after the Christmas holiday season about molting birds. In almost every case, it turns out that the bird in question is kept in a dining or living room and due to the holiday season has been exposed to more hours of light than it is accustomed to because its owners stay awake longer than usual or entertain later. If this situation occurs, simply remove the canary from the area at the time he normally goes to sleep and place him in a darkened bedroom or other area where he will not be exposed to light. (Even the flickering light from a television can be enough to keep him awake.) If this is not possible, cover the cage with a dark cloth which is heavy enough to prevent light from penetrating.

I also often hear from people who have gone on vacation and left a bird with someone who is on a different schedule from the family. Even if the bird receives the same number of hours of light, it is important that he remain on his normal schedule. This can easily be accomplished with lights on timers.

Any change in lighting must be made gradually and with the understanding that it could cause a molt. My birds- and every line of canaries is different- are maintained at 9 to 9½ hours of light except during show and breeding season. During show season, the hours of light are increased to 10 to 10 ½ hours depending on how the birds are singing. Breeding season is brought on in part by increasing the length of day in 15 minute increments twice per week until the birds reach a maximum of 14 hours of light each day. After breeding is finished, the light is increased suddenly to 15 hours for a day or two and then dropped to 9 hours all at once. Within a week, every bird in the room will begin to molt. The few older birds which lag behind will have a tail feather or two pulled and that will generally bring them into the molt as well. This certainly does not work for every breeder- some canary breeds (and even individual birds) require more light to breed and thus would resist molting at higher day lengths. This does show how sensitive the canary is to light, however.

If a canary is taken from a place where he receives ten hours of light and placed in a home where he suddenly is exposed to fifteen hours, chances are excellent that he will molt. The same is true of the reverse. Sometimes even a half-hour difference will cause a problem, so a new pet owner should inquire about a new bird's schedule before bringing him home.

Generally, male canaries kept as pets should awaken with the sun and go to sleep with the sun- this lighting schedule will provide the easiest way for a pet owner to avoid unseasonable molting problems.

The second largest problem pet bird owners have is heat- too much warmth will almost invariably cause a canary to molt. Remember that despite hundreds of years of domestication, a canary is still a wild bird in biological terms with all the hardwired switches intact. When his body is exposed to warmth, a canary's brain screams "MOLT!" Whether this is increasing warmth due to the season or an environment that is always kept too warm, the effect is largely the same.

Sometimes it simply isn't possible to avoid keeping a bird in a warm environment, such as during the summer. Summertime warmth isn't a problem, since the bird should molt at this time of year anyway. Often, though, unseasonable molting is brought on by keeping a bird near a ceiling (which can be several degrees warmer than nearer the floor), close to furnace vents, in a warm kitchen, or near an electric space heater.

A bird which is kept in front of a window must always have an area of his cage where he can escape direct sunlight to avoid becoming overheated- simply covering a portion of the cage with a cloth will suffice. On very hot, sunny days moving the cage away from the window entirely will be helpful as the sun's rays are intensified by the glass.

The third problem that can cause a pet bird to molt is exposure to a draft which is substantially different in temperature from that of the room in which he is kept-regardless of whether it is hot, warm or cold. Some drafts are obvious, such as those coming in from a window or a heating or air-conditioning vent. Others are less so- air blowing from a fan can be redirected off of objects in the room directly onto the bird. Birds need fresh air, so an open window is good as long as the bird is protected and allowed a sheltered perching area in his cage which is free of draft.

A male canary will most likely not sing as long as he is molting and for a short period after he appears to have finished. Singing in the canary is determined in large part by hormone levels, which are decreased during the molt. If the bird has received good nutrition and is healthy he will certainly begin to sing again.

The molting season is an excellent time to play recorded canary song CDs and cassette tapes as it is theorized that canaries learn new songs best during this period.

There are many ideas about ways to stop a molt once it has begun, but it is very difficult to accomplish and not healthy for the bird. Battling against a bird's biological nature is a fight which is lost before it has begun! The best way to avoid untimely molting is to manage the environment so that it doesn't occur.

Exhibition

Judging of the American Singer Song

The song of a great American Singer canary cannot be rivaled; free-flowing, interesting, and pleasing to the ear, the song is a welcome addition to any household. What makes an American Singer song unique is its very uniqueness- unlike the song of other canaries bred for singing ability, the American Singer has no song standard. It is not required to sing particular tours in the twenty minute judging period- only to sing fully, freely and with good variety, tone, showmanship, and overall quality.

Many fanciers of other breeds of song canaries have the incorrect perception that American Singer judging is based purely on a judge's personal preference due to lack of an official song standard. While it is true that certain judges have a particular sound or quality they prefer, a great bird will place under many different judges. This is illustrated by results from the annual Quad shows in California, where the same birds will turn up again and again in the top six places under different judges.

Something that critics fail to take into account is that the American Singer canary is a reflection of the country of its origin- democratic, egalitarian, continuously evolving, and valuing freedom and personal achievement over bloodlines and rigid conformity to a particular system. The thing which many criticize the breed for is the same one which attracts so many fanciers that the breed is capable of supporting more than thirty American Singer sections a year across the U.S. - far more than any other song breed. It is possible for a novice with a basic understanding of song to begin winning at shows with American Singers without the lengthy study of notes, tours, score sheets, and pedigrees required to master the breeding of rollers, waterslagers, and timbrados. As with all subjects however, study improves performance. For this reason a discussion of American Singer judging would be of assistance to the novice as well as to those seeking a greater understanding of song judging.

The Score
The American Singer is judged on a 100-point scoring system, which breaks down this way: Song, a total of 70 points may be earned- 10 points for Freedom (one point for each complete song), 60 points for Rendition; Conformation, a total of 20 points; and Condition, a total of 10 points.

The judging period is 20 minutes long and is subdivided into two 10 minute segments- the first is called the freedom period and the second the rendition period. During the freedom period birds are awarded one point for each complete song they sing- cheeps, trills, and call notes are not counted- to a maximum of 10 points. According to the American Singer constitution, birds which do not sing during this period can receive points for freedom if they sing during the second 10 minute rendition period but common practice among judges is to not award freedom points for singing during the rendition portion as a bird which does not sing early fails to meet the basic qualification of being a free singer. The second 10 minute portion of the judging period is called the rendition period. It is during this period that the song itself is evaluated. (Although in reality song evaluation begins as soon as a bird begins to sing on the bench.) Evaluation of the song includes issues such as tone, volume, variety, and range. Shrillness, harshness, excessive chopping (defined as more than six chops sung in a row; some chopping is expected due to the American Singer's Border ancestry), and other faults cause deductions to be made to the rendition score. Freedom plays an essential role in the rendition period as a bird who does not sing often cannot be fully evaluated.

Conformation, which accounts for a maximum of 20 points, refers to how well the bird conforms to the physical model. Points are lost under conformation for crossed wings, skinny bodies, flat heads, missing toes, fish tails, size, plumage, and similar issues. In practice, faults such as missing body parts are sometimes deducted under condition but in these cases the bird is really failing to conform to the breed standard- which includes two eyes, eight toes, etc. One point is deducted for each fault. Color is irrelevant and is not considered under conformation.

Condition accounts for a maximum of 10 points and considers issues such as apparent health, vigor, cleanliness of both bird and cage, and conformity of cage setup to standard. Points are deducted for dirty plumage; long toenails, missing bottom perches, incorrectly sized or misplaced perches, etc.

As outlined in the ASC Constitution, ties are broken by conformation and condition scores.

Rendition
The rendition score is the judge's overall evaluation of the song. This score can be a cause for both confusion on the part of novices and a source of contention for experienced exhibitors. One thing that every exhibitor should be aware of is that birds sound very differently from the position of the judge's table. Having sat there myself as I begin preparation to become qualified for my judging card, I can attest to the fact that a few feet of distance between the birds and the listeners can make a world of difference in what is heard.

Rendition can be defined simply as a musical performance. Judgment of musical performance is inherently subjective but judges- as do all good music critics- have certain values in mind when critiquing song. These include, but are not limited to: volume, tone, range, variety, melodiousness, and showmanship.

An American Singer should be neither too loud nor too soft. This is quite obviously very subjective (and highly sensitive to variables such as the acoustics of the judging room, the relative volume of other birds in a class, etc.). In broad terms, a bird which overpowers all the other birds in the room is too loud and one which cannot make himself heard is too soft.

Tone is defined as music or sound with reference to its pitch, quality, and strength. To those who prefer a simple explanation- such as myself- this refers to the bird's ability to sing on key with a beautiful, strong, rich fullness to the song. A bird without good tone can sing the best song ever produced by a canary, but it just doesn't *sound good*.

Range refers to the lowest and highest pitches a bird can sing. Rollers sing in the low range while borders tend to sing in the high range. An American Singer should be able to sing both low and high notes.

Variety in simplest terms refers to the collection of distinct notes, tours, or song passages the bird sings. A bird which repeats the same limited number of notes and passages over and over again lacks variety. The term variety could also be used to more broadly describe the way in which a bird mixes the notes and tours- singing notes one way and then another and changing the order of passages and tours.

Melodiousness refers to the pleasing, harmonic way the bird puts his song together. The song should flow from one passage to another in a pleasant, coherent stream of sound rather than bounce from one sound to the next with little connection.

Showmanship is a vital part of the American Singer's performance. Often the major difference between a Grand Champion and a good singer is that the Grand Champion puts on a show- he is proud of his song and wants to be heard. He will not stand on the bottom perch, hide behind a water or seed cup, stand on the floor of the show cage- he perches confidently on a top perch, looks the judge in the eye, and *sings*. The judge cannot help but notice a bird who is a good showman.

Good judges will include notes about both positive and negative aspects of the bird's song to assist the exhibitor in developing a clear understanding of the bird's strengths and weaknesses. Judges, like music critics, have personal preferences- some prefer louder or softer volume, longer songs, wider range, or place heavy emphasis on tone but every judge notices quality song. Knowing the sound of the birds the judge breeds him or herself does not guarantee that an exhibitor will be able to predict with any certainty what the judge will choose. The one guaranteed thing that will grab any judge's attention is a truly exceptional song.

Preparing for Your First Show

Getting Ready!

As the Boy Scouts' motto goes, be prepared! Traveling with birds is much easier if one has everything one needs on hand. Every exhibitor has their own kit and method, but I have found this one to work for me.

Supplies for Showing

- Show cages- clean and repainted as necessary.
- An extra empty show cage can be a lifesaver!
- A large plastic toolbox to carry everything in. I prefer the toolbox, but I've seen everything used from diaper bags to cardboard boxes- if it works for you, use it!
- Extra top and long perches to replace those which become soiled.
- Extra drinkers and feeders to replace any that might be broken.
- A supply of plain, white paper cut to fit the cage bottom (10 ½ inches by 6 3/4 inches). Some shows supply cage paper, but most do not.
- A container of drinking water- the quality of the water is never certain, always bring some from home.
- Plenty of seed mix- always bring extra!
- An assortment of Ziploc-style plastic bags to put dirty perches and drinkers in for the trip home. A Ziploc bag also makes a handy place to dump drinkers if you have to set up your birds far from a sink.
- Scissors.
- Nail clippers.
- Band cutters- just in case of an emergency.
- Bird net- birds do get loose and few shows have one on hand.
- Baby wipes for spot-cleaning cages.
- Registration sheet- completed prior to leaving home, if possible. It's handy to have several of these in one's show kit. Complete the form by supplying your name and address, band numbers, etc. before you go to the show as once at the show things can become hectic and having it filled out before you leave home gives you one less thing to worry about at the show.
- Stapler for stapling shut show tags.
- Mailing labels are handy for using in show tags as they save a lot of writing, but they must be very small.
- Paper or plastic grocery sacks for throwing away soiled cage papers, seed, etc. as there

is usually a shortage of garbage cans.

- Large polyester duffel bags- I am forever indebted to a fellow American Singer fancier who showed me the extra large bags she had purchased at a large retail store for $15 each. These bags are large enough to carry four show cages in and can be zipped closed if using the old Herbst-style cages. The new Prevue-Hendryx cages are larger and the zipper will not close if you place four cages in each bag, but the top can be left open and a pillowcase used to cover the opening. The bags are lightweight, washable, and easy to store when not in use.

Supplies for Selling Birds
- Boxes or paper sacks in which to send sale birds home with their new owners.
- Pedigree sheets for each sale bird.
- Breeding records.
- Business cards.

Supplies for the Exhibitor
- Directions to the show hall and to the hotel/motel (and directions for getting from one to the other!)
- Hotel phone number, street address and reservation confirmation information.
- Phone number for the show manager or other designated contact person for the club hosting the show.
- Clothing, medication, and other personal needs items.
- Notebook or clipboard for taking notes about birds.
- Pencils and pens.
- Camera and supplies.
- Carry a list of the band numbers of all the birds you bring to the show- including those being sold.
- Always be prepared for bad weather- drive safely and stay an extra night if necessary!

At the Show

Benching- Entering Birds

Be sure that all your supplies will fit inside your vehicle before loading the birds. If the weather is cold or bad be sure to cover the birds well for the trip from the house to the car. When packing, ensure that the cages are packed securely and will not shift.

Plan your trip so you arrive at the show hall early. Should you get lost along the way, this will allow you time to make it to the show hall before benching closes for the evening. If not, being there early will give you plenty of time to prepare your birds. This also makes life less stressful for the show secretary, who typically prefers exhibitors to arrive early to avoid last-minute shuffling of classes to fit late-coming birds in.

It is usually best to go to the show hall before you check into the hotel. After bringing your birds and supplies into the hall, see the show secretary to drop off your completed registration form (or to pick one up). While the secretary is completing your show tags, set up your birds- make sure all the perches are clean and properly placed, all feed and water cups are filled, and cage papers are clean. Secure the cage door and tray in the manner the particular show requires (each show may use a different color of pipe cleaner or even rubber bands). After the secretary has completed your show tags, you must secure them to the front left corner of the appropriate show cage- each tag is assigned to a particular bird- and staple each tag shut. Be sure to ask for assistance with this your first time if you have any questions because you'll have to do it all over again if you make a mistake!

Once cages are ready, simply stack them in the holding room. The show secretary will randomly assign each cage number to a particular class and the cages will then be grouped according to class in the holding area. After all classes are separated and checked, they will be covered with white sheets and the lights in the holding area are turned off so the birds can sleep.

The judge determines what time judging will begin in the morning. It is not required to be present when judging begins- the first show at which I exhibited, I returned to the show hall at 7am as I was told that was when the judging began. For over an hour, the only folks present were the judge, the show secretary, and myself!

Show Day

When the judge arrives in the morning, he or she will determine the order of classes by a random drawing of the class letters. For this reason, the show secretary will not be able to tell you when your birds' classes will be until the morning of the show. After the classes have been drawn, the show secretary will create a chart listing the class order (and the cage numbers of all birds assigned to that class) and post it in a public area. As birds are judged, the 1ˢᵗ through 3ʳᵈ place class winners are posted on this chart.

In the following example, classes of old birds are assigned a single uppercase letter and young birds are assigned double lowercase letters.

Number	Class	Cage Numbers	1st Place	2nd Place	3rd Place
1	A	03, 13, 27, 41, 52, 57	52	13	03
2	ss	12, 31, 32, 40, 77, 101, 107	12	77	31
3	cc	01, 02, 11, 24, 33, 37, 51	51	33	01

On the copy of your registration form you were given by the show secretary, note the classes your birds are in and the number so you may listen to them if you wish.

If the number of entries is large, the judging will continue for some time. You are welcome to sit in the room during judging (at the judge's discretion) as long as you are quiet and stay for the entire twenty minute period.

This is also a good time to familiarize yourself with the show environment and to learn more about preparing your birds for exhibition. Take the time to visit with other breeders and exhibitors, check out the birds at the sales tables, and participate in the show raffle. Be sure to listen to the birds who have taken places in their classes! Most experienced breeders welcome questions from novices and are happy to offer pointers about breeding and showing.

After the show, be careful when packing up your birds. Check each bird off on your registration form as you pack it away for the trip home to ensure that you don't forget one. When you arrive home, ensure that the birds receive extra good nutrition and are kept quiet for a few days. Showing is stressful and they will need time to recover.

Quick Tips for the Show Novice

- Arriving early for benching is always preferable to arriving late for both the exhibitor and the show secretary.
- It takes some time for show tags to be made up. The show secretary will usually call out for you when they are ready.
- The show secretary is generally in charge of entering birds and copying score sheets on behalf of the judge. In addition, while the judge is officially in charge of what is going on at the show- he or she is responsible for ensuring that the show is conducted fairly and in accordance with the ASC constitution- the show secretary is also unofficially responsible for ensuring that the show is conducted properly.
- Once the birds are benched, or placed into classes, they cannot be removed from cages by exhibitors (to wash feet or tails, for example) except when requested to do so by a judge checking a leg band.
- Once benched, no one but show officials may touch or move cages.
- Birds may be entered in shows for song score only- always check with the show secretary as to how this should be noted when registering. Birds entered for score only are not eligible for prizes or awards. Some shows do have special tutor sections in which purchased birds may be entered for judging. If offered, these sections are usually listed in the show catalog.
- Peeking at the show tags is not allowed! Tags cannot be opened until after the show.
- Quiet should be maintained as much as possible in the holding and judging areas- whenever possible move away from these areas to talk to folks.
- No peeking beneath the sheets!
- Birds may not be sold until released from the bench.
- Birds cannot be packed up or removed from the show hall until all the birds are released from the bench by the judge.
- When in the judging room, turn off all cell phones and pagers. Be sure to remain seated and silent until the judge indicates that you may speak. Judges have the authority to ask anyone interfering with judging in any way to leave.
- Neither the judge nor the show secretary will release scores until the winners have been announced. Score sheets are not released until after the birds are released from the bench.
- Certain rules vary from show to show- usually these are discussed in the show catalog. Sometimes judging will end on Saturday but birds may not be taken until Sunday, for example.
- When in doubt, never hesitate to ask!

American Singer Show Cages

The American Singer show cage was adopted in 1938. In the intervening years it has been made by a variety of companies and both older and new models are permitted.

Prevue Hendryx show cages- the only new show cages currently available- are 10½ inches wide, 7 inches deep, and 10½ inches high. The right side is solid metal and the top and sides are wire.

New cages can be purchased from Prevue Hendryx in cases of three. The model is LP, which is described as a breeding cage but is actually a show cage. 2005 pricing is $73.50 per case plus shipping. Cages can be ordered by calling 800/243-3624. New cages are generally outfitted with the torpedo-style drinker and seed cup shown in the illustration but the majority of exhibitors use glass or plastic cups which are available from Abba Products Corporation (telephone 908/353-0669).

Cage paper is to be white and clean. Unlike other types of canary breeds, no seed mix is dumped on the bottom of the cage.

Perches must be round and ½ inch diameter. Each cage must have two short perches placed to either side of the door and a long "feeder" perch. (In certain areas of the country the custom has become to place the perches over the door rather than to either side- acceptance of this custom varies from judge to judge.) Food cups should be located on the left side while water is located on the right.

No marked cages are allowed- these are cages which have a distinctive mark, decoration, or other feature by which one cage could be distinguished from another. All cages must be nickel or silver finish and black cage trays are now permitted.

American Singer Show Cage,
Prevue Hendryx Model

American Singer Training Tips and Tricks

Show Cage Preparation

- New show cages should be washed thoroughly and left in the sun to dry. The Prevue Hendryx label should be removed with an adhesive removal product or by using a hair dryer to melt the glue. New show cages are very shiny and males can end up singing to their own reflection so the solid side should be sanded lightly to dull the finish.
- Older show cages may need to be repainted with nontoxic silver or aluminum spray paint. A number of different products have been recommended to me over the years but in my experience almost all of them rub off on the tails of light birds despite rubbing the cages down before placing birds in them. The only remedy for this is to follow up the colored spray with a clear coat. All cages should be allowed to air dry for several days to a week before using.
- While it is permitted to use the torpedo tubes provided by Prevue Hendryx with new cages in the shows, in practice most exhibitors use the plastic or glass cups. The plastic cups can be purchased new. The glass cups can be purchased for $1 to $2 each from exhibitors who are downsizing or retiring.
- If you choose to use the plastic or glass cups, the cage wires must be spread to allow their placement. The correct positioning of them is between the 3rd and 4th wires from each end on the front of the cage.

Caging Up

- Males should usually be caged up three to four weeks before the date of their first show. Some fanciers cage birds up sooner, but care should be taken to ensure that the birds do not become "cage fatigued".
- Birds which have been seen singing in the flight are caged up first. Once in a while a late bloomer will surface in the flight after all the other males have been caged up, so be sure to continue listening for birds in the flight even after the others are in show cages.
- The band number of each bird should be placed on the outside of the cage for easy reference. This can be easily done by using the plastic bag clips from bread, vegetables, etc. Simply write the band number in indelible marker on the plastic tag and clip on the front of the cage.
- Each male should have his toenails trimmed prior to placing in the show cage.
- When caging birds up, turn the cages so the birds can see each other. After they have settled down, the cages should be turned so that the birds cannot see their neighbors.
- Most birds will not sing in the cages on the first day, though a few brave little souls may.
- For the first few days, birds should be carefully watched to make sure they find the

water and the food cups. Even older birds that have been caged up before sometimes forget how to drink from the cups and can become dehydrated. Some breeders provide plastic tube waterers near the top perches in addition to the water cups.

- For some reason, birds sometimes forget how to drink from the cups even after they've been drinking for some time from them. If any bird looks dehydrated- blinking frequently or developing constipation- place a water tube in the cage right away.
- I do not place the long perches in the Herbst-style show cages until the birds go to the show as they simply become soiled; using newer models of show cages will necessitate the use of the long perches as the cups rest higher up from the cage floor. Birds do not seem to have any difficulty with eating or drinking from the floor in the old style cages, but they should be monitored to make sure they can reach both. I scatter a little seed on the floor of the cage for the first day or so.
- Birds can be sprayed every few days with warm water mixed with a teaspoonful or so of Listerine in a spray bottle to maintain the luster of the plumage.
- When birds are training, reversing the seed and water cups can prevent the birds from splattering the solid side of the cage when they bathe in the water cup.
- Place several sheets of plain white typing paper in the tray- using newspaper will result in dirty-looking feathers. Some breeders do not cut the paper to size but leave the extra sticking out from the front of the tray; this extra paper will catch some of the seed birds throw out of the cage.
- A long- time breeder suggests taping trays closed to prevent accidental injury to birds when moving cages. I have also seen large rubber bands used to secure cage trays. The tray can slide out and toes or legs can be broken.
- Show cages should be cleaned every day and soiled perches replaced with clean ones. The more often cages are handled, the better- this way birds become accustomed to jostling. Don't avoid bumping the cages around- a gentle bang or two to remove seeds from the bottom of the cage won't hurt the bird.
- Unlike some breeders, I do not cage my birds up until they are in full song as mine are usually in full song in August. Breeders who use natural lighting will find that they have a number of birds are still in baby song in early September and will be caging up these as well. Birds which are heavily molting in the first part of September will not be ready until quite late in the show season, if they don't miss the show season entirely.
- Birds which do not sing after a week in a show cage are likely hens.

Quick and Easy Show Training
- Show training should take about three weeks. Many feel it takes a month or more, but three weeks can be more than sufficient to provide effective training if one has stock with sufficient freedom and time to devote to intensive training.
- The purpose of training is to accustom birds to some of the things they will experience at the shows- being sheeted down, moved around, and exposed to a variety of different

sounds and songs. Many will state that the purpose of training is to teach birds to sing on command, but freedom cannot be trained- it must be bred into birds. If birds are bred for freedom and have the extroverted, steady personality expected in an American Singer, the birds will require less training than those with less freedom and shyer personalities. Even the freest singer needs exposure to different situations to perform well at the shows, however.

- After one has one's males caged up and has given them a day or so to adjust (sometimes a little longer if they are being moved from a large walk-in flight directly to the show cages), then birds are ready to begin training. As Judy Snider wrote in her article "The Way of the Champion," "training begins when the male ceases to fear his solitude in the show cage". Attempting to train before birds have settled down will merely prolong training.

- The key to good training is to teach the bird that the unexpected will not hurt or kill him. Most canaries will not believe this at first and they will freeze or fly around frantically in the cage every time something new occurs.

- When cleaning the show cages, they should never be placed back in the same position but changed around so that the bird has to learn to adjust to a new place and new neighbors every day. Be sure to shuffle the bird's position from top to bottom if cages are stacked, too.

- Male canaries sing to define territory- healthy birds in good physical condition should sing each time they are placed somewhere new.

- Birds should be covered with sheets occasionally. Some recommend keeping the birds covered all the time and removing sheets three or four times a day for a half hour or so until the males sing reliably within five minutes of sheeting. I prefer to keep the birds guessing and sheet them down intermittently. I shake the sheet in front of the cages and even use sheets of different colors once in a while.

- Ideally, one should set up an area where birds can be placed under different types of lighting- fluorescent (full spectrum AND regular), natural, and incandescent. Every show has a different lighting setup in the judging room and this is one of the things most often overlooked in show training. Birds which are well trained under fluorescent light fixtures may freeze under lighting from bare fluorescent bulbs (and vice versa) - exposing them to as many different kinds of lighting as possible will help to prevent this.

- Another thing people sometimes fail to take into account when training birds is the environment in the judging room. The judging room is silent and filled with strange people doing nothing but watching the birds. This situation can seriously unnerve a bird accustomed to a noisy, busy bird room with few human visitors but the breeder. Allow birds to experience extremely quiet places and, if possible, engage some people to sit and stare at the birds.

- Cages should be placed in the crates or boxes in which they will be transported and carried up and down stairs, around the house, and loaded into and out of the car.

- A television can be a helpful training tool, especially if tuned to programs with lots of different sound levels and action. If you use a television to assist in training, you will see that initially the birds will become startled easily by many of the unusual sounds but as they become accustomed to it they will startle much less often and settle down much more quickly afterwards. It has been reported that Cliff Williams always played a television for his birds, and no one can dispute his success!
- Song tapes and CDs are great during training- not so much for teaching song but for getting the birds used to hearing foreign song.
- Tutors are often used for teaching- to be most effective, the tutor should be from the young bird's line and have a similar song.
- Tutors are used during the training period not only for teaching but also to get singing started. The danger in this is that one is fostering dependency on the tutor- ideally, a bird should begin to sing right away without the stimulus of another singer.
- Keep the birds off balance as much as possible throughout the training period- teaching them to expect the unexpected is the goal of training!
- When birds sing, mark their cages with a small red-colored sticky dot.
- Arrange listening sessions so that you can evaluate your birds- it is difficult to accurately gauge the quality of singing by listening while performing bird room chores. Set the birds up in groups of five to seven (sometimes more if the birds are not all singing) and listen for 20-30 minutes. Each bird should have as many listening sessions as possible.
- Keep notes on each bird- include such items as freedom, variety notes, faults, tone quality, and showmanship.
- Make notes about each bird and cull birds that are in full song and are shrill or obviously lacking in variety or tone. Culled birds receive a special color sticky dot to denote "sale bird status." (Be very careful at this stage as it is easy to mistakenly sell good birds.)

- Some fanciers make song cards for each bird which something look like this:

Bird Band No.	Caged Up:	Sibling's Band Numbers:
Freedom: Tone:	Variety:	
Faults:		
Notes:		

- Make hash marks in the freedom section during evaluation periods.
- Keeping careful notes will allow you to refresh your memory and help you to avoid selling birds you wished to keep!
- Be sure to note the band numbers of siblings who are hens to avoid selling the sisters of good singers.

Before The Shows Begin
- Wash feet and tails a few days before the show.
- Remove colored plastic leg bands.
- Be sure to keep moving the birds and rearranging stacks of cages, playing tapes of strange bird song, and generally keeping the birds sharp.
- Pack the show box.
- Expect 50% of the young birds to receive a NS for "no song" at their first show. This percentage should decrease with each successive show.

Notes on Maintaining Training during the Shows:
- I have found canaries to have very, very short memories. During the show season when a break of some time presents itself, the temptation is to release birds back into the flights or into breeding cages. Some fanciers do this and have no problems, but in my experience male left in flights for more than a day forget their training quickly. I release my birds into tabletop flights for no more than half a day to exercise and take a bath

about once a week.

- Most males who got along well in the flights when they were young will fight with each other after they have been caged separately. Some breeders do release their males into a single flight cage between shows without any problem, but in general once males have been caged up in show cages, the only time they should be caged together again is when they are molting heavily and are turned into the flight.

Glossary of Some Common American Singer Show Terms

Benching- grouping of birds into classes.

Buff/Frosted- any feather color, tips of feathers are white producing a softer, "downier" feather.

Cinnamon- yellow ground color, warm reddish-brown color.

Clear- any ground color, refers to lack of pigmentation. Example: a clear yellow bird is one with no visible variegation.

Condition- health, vigor and stamina. Also refers to the cleanliness of the bird and the cage.

Conformation- adherence to the physical standards regarding feather quality, size, wings, tail, carriage, etc.

Cross Wings- wings which cross at the tip.

Fawn- white ground bird, color is a very light cinnamon brown.

Fish Tail- very broad tail with a "v" at the tip.

Flat Head- Head which is flattened, with little dome.

Foul- dark bird with one or two light feathers in the wing flights or tail.

Freedom- per the ASC constitution: "willingness to sing; ease in starting and in performance".

Green: all dark bird.

Hard Feathered- brighter color, tighter feathers with no frosting present. Hard feathered birds may appear smaller-bodied than buff birds due to the tightness of their feathers.

Heavy Variegated (HV) - at least 75% dark, but less than 100%.

Hooping (or Roller Hoop) - sings with head stretched out and body curved in an arc.

Light Variegated (LV) - less than 50% dark markings.

Medium Variegated (MV) - between 50% and 75% dark markings.

No Song (NS) - The bird did not sing during the twenty minute judging period.

Red Factor- birds which carry the red factor gene inherited from the Siskin. This term is often misused- red factor refers to the gene(s) which cause(s) birds to express red coloration; the term "red" or "red ground" should be used to refer to these birds.

Rendition- overall performance of the song.

Show Manager- responsible for the overall organization of the show.

Show Secretary- person responsible for registering birds, grouping entries into classes, transcribing of judge's class sheets onto exhibitor score sheets and a number of other functions.

Show Stewards- host club members assigned to care for benched birds, move classes of birds as needed and other responsibilities as necessary.

Self- refers to blues, greens, cinnamons and fawns. All dark, no light feathers.

Snake Head- shapeless head with no roundness and a long beak.

Song- per the ASC constitution, "a musical sequence of notes and tours".

Strength- does not refer to loudness but to the power with which the song is sung.

Thin Neck- having too much break in the neck between the base of the skull and the shoulder.

Ticked- any color bird; dark marking smaller than a dime (two ticked marks would be a lightly variegated bird).

Miscellaneous

Handy Things to Have on Hand in the Birdroom

General Supplies

- Listerine- add to bathing water for its antibacterial properties. It adds a nice luster to the feathers and it is also said to discourage mites.
- Apple Cider Vinegar- add to bathing water to add luster to feathers. It is said to provide some gastrointestinal benefits in that it can be used to acidify the gut and treat intestinal disturbances.
- Good quality vitamin and mineral supplement- to ensure that birds do not have vitamin or mineral deficiencies. If using a vitamized seed this should not be used to avoid vitamin overdosing.
- Oxyfresh all-purpose detergent- a mild cleaner with a pleasant scent that removes dried bird droppings better than anything else I have tried. A gallon lasts a very long time and it is completely nontoxic. Oxyfresh now has a super-concentrated disinfectant product called Dent-A-Gene which promises to be even better in the aviary.
- Bleach- original strength, not the ultra strength. Used to disinfect perches, dishes, etc.
- Hand sanitizer- wash hands thoroughly and use sanitizer after handling sick birds or those in quarantine.
- Masking tape- handy for taping down cage papers and nest liners as well as covering up frequently soiled parts of cages. When the tape becomes dirty, simply tear it off and apply clean tape!
- Split plastic bands in assorted colors for identification of birds in flights.
- Red split plastic bands to identify males.
- Plastic organizer with a number of compartments for storing small odds and ends like bands, nail clippers, etc.
- Wooden spring-type clothespins- they can be used for holding vegetables, stabilizing perches, holding rope perching, making individual perches in the flight for young males to practice song, and much more.
- "S" hooks for hanging cages from other cages such as when introducing males to hens. I also use them to hang show cages on the wire mesh of the walk-in flight during the training period- inside the flight with a clothespin to hold the door open when getting the birds accustomed to being inside the show cage and on the outside of the flight to save space after all the young males are caged up in the fall.
- Paper plates- use for feeding soft food, vegetables, and fruits. Don't use foam plates as the birds pick at them and may ingest the foam.

- Toys of various types to keep juvenile birds occupied.
- Rolls of white, unscented toilet paper to hang in the flight and give birds something to pick at other than their neighbor's feathers.
- A freezer to store seed and other foods in for the birds.
- Access to a sink to get water and to wash bird things.
- A shop vacuum to clean up seed and feathers.

Medical Supplies

- A small pair of cuticle scissors for trimming vent feathers, cutting small fibers which have become entangled around toes, and removing plastic identification bands.
- A magnifying glass to examine birds with.
- Tweezers.
- Human fingernail clippers for trimming nails and beaks.
- Band cutter (an absolute must-have).
- Styptic powder or cornstarch for stopping bleeding.
- Pepto Bismol- one drop into the beak to treat diarrhea.
- Kaopectate- one drop into the beak to treat constipation.
- Antibiotic ointment.
- Rubbing alcohol.
- Frontline spray (0.29% fipronil) - one small drop applied with an eyedropper on or near the preen gland can be used every 2-3 months to prevent or treat mites.
- Cotton swabs- to apply medications (and also to clean out hard to reach areas in the birdroom).
- Artificial tears or sterile saline solution- to wash eyes.
- Powdered Pedialyte- to provide fluid and electrolytes to sick birds who have become or who are at risk of becoming dehydrated.
- Betadine solution- for treatment of wounds.
- Eyedroppers.
- Heating pad.
- Small cage to be used for housing sick birds.
- Ivermectin- 1 cc of 1% ivermectin solution per 32 oz water is the dosage recommended by Dr. Abbate of ABBA seed. Ivomec Sheep Drench .08% formula can also be used. The dosage for the .08% formula is 20 ml to each liter of fresh water.

During Breeding Season

- A plastic container of the sort with small individual compartments makes a handy place to store eggs when pulling them. Number each breeding cage with a unique number and then label each compartment with a number. As eggs are laid, be sure to place each egg in the appropriately numbered place to ensure that each hen receives her own eggs when the hens are set. Compartments can be filled with rolled oats or stale seed to cushion the eggs.

- Unscented talc- this is much better to use than oil, hand soap, etc. when banding chicks with closed leg bands as it allows the band to slide easily over the foot but does not make the bird's leg greasy.
- Extra cages to place birds in who do not cohabitate well with their mates.
- Small cages which can be hung on the side of a breeding cage to place chicks in who are being plucked but are not yet self-supporting. Parents will continue to feed chicks through the wires of the cages as long as the cages are placed tightly together. A bird bath also works as long as it is large enough to allow the chicks room to move around and it is lined with nesting material.
- Commercial hand feeding formula for feeding chicks. This can be frozen for quite some time to preserve freshness and is more nutritious than most homemade hand feeding formulas. These formulas also include helpful instructions and educational material about hand feeding birds.
- 3 inch x 5 inch index cards to keep breeding records on and to make individual records for each chick. Colored cards allow coding by year of hatch. A card file to keep them in prevents wear.
- A safe place to store closed leg bands. Nothing is more nerve wracking than to lose leg bands during breeding season and have to order more!

Lighting Schedule

This is the schedule used in my birdroom, which has all natural light blocked year-round. Lights are kept on electric timers which permit increases of any length- many lamp timers permit increases in 30 minute intervals only. If using this type of timer, increase the duration of lighting one time per week rather than twice a week.

This schedule works for my lines of American Singer canaries- other lines and breeds may have different requirements. Many breeders report that their birds need more than fourteen hours of light to breed while I stay at fourteen hours or less- more than this and some birds will certainly begin dropping feathers.

Using this schedule birds should be ready by the beginning of January for breeding.

Date	Hours of Light	Comments
September 1	9 hours	Birds have been maintained on this level all summer long.
1st weekend in September	9.25 hours	Beginning this week, duration of light is increased by 15 minutes per week to bring birds into full song for show season by the first weekend in October.
1st weekend in October through the last weekend in November	10 hours	Birds should be in full song; if not, increase duration by 15 minutes per week until they are. Bear in mind that breeding song is not permitted on the show bench- keeping birds in full song but not singing breeding song is part of the challenge of showing!

1st weekend in December	10.25- 10.5 hours	The number of hours birds are on at this point depends on how they were singing in the shows. My birds sing well if kept on no more than 11 hours- more than that and they begin coming into breeding condition.
2nd weekend in December	11 hours	Duration of lighting is increased by 15 minutes twice a week from this time until the end of December. Lighting intensity should also be increased by using additional bulbs in fixtures or adding lights. Some hens begin dropping eggs at 11.5 hours- they are not paired up but allowed to recycle until 13 hours.
End of December	12 hours	Birds are beginning to show signs of coming into breeding condition- hens are tearing paper, males are singing lustily and all birds are much more active. Light intensity should be fairly bright.
Mid January	13 hours	Birds are paired up. Hens go straight to building nests and mating occurs frequently. Should birds seem behind, increase lighting duration by 15 minutes until they come into full condition.
Mid February	13.5 hours	Laggardly birds should be in breeding condition by this time. Pairs are feeding chicks.

3rd week of February	13.5 to14 hours	I do not push my birds too much beyond this point during the breeding season as some will tend to begin molting.
Middle of April	13.5 to 14 hours	If birds were permitted to go two rounds, breeding season should be nearing an end.1st round babies are coming into the baby molt and beginning to drop feathers.
End of April	14 hours	2nd round babies are weaned and self supporting. Song tapes and CDs are played all day while the lights are on.
Early May	14 hours	All babies are in the walk-in flight and are eating well.
2nd weekend in May	9 hours	Duration of lights is dropped to 9 hours all at once.
Last weekend in May	9 hours	Most birds are showing signs of molting. Older birds which are not molting are caught and several tail feathers are pulled.
2nd weekend in June	9 hours	If males appear to be in full molt, they are placed in the large aviary with the hens and young birds.
End of June	9 hours	All birds are well into the molt. 1st round babies may be finished. The aviary begins to get a little noisier as young birds start twittering and singing baby song.

July through September 1	9 hours	Lights are maintained at this duration until show training begins in September.

Show Score Records
for the Year _____

SHOW Chapter, Location & Date	(Example) Chapter 32, Cleveland October 8					
Judge	M. Smith					
Band No.	Song Score/Total Score					
(EXAMPLE) C830-04	54 / 92					

Show Notes

Canary Related Sites on the Web

I am an insatiable reader and am always looking for new information about canaries, their care, breeding, and almost anything else regarding them. These are the sites I use when I need information about canaries.

General Canary Information and Care

My own website dedicated to the breeding and exhibition of American Singer canaries. www.americansingercanary.com

One of the best-known canary sites on the web. Frequently updated, the site provides a host of high quality information and resources for everyone from pet owners to breeders. www.robirda.com

Site providing interesting information about the care of parrots and other exotic birds. www.birdsnways.com

Information about song type canaries. www.gis.net/~ruben/song.html

Canary List Info Pages- lists of canary web pages, bird web pages, mail order suppliers- lots more! Infrequently updated, but a valuable resource nonetheless. www.members.aol.com/CanaryList

Helpful articles about canaries and other birds. www.birds2grow.com/Articles.html

Wonderful articles about birds and lighting. www.users.mis.net/~pthrush/lighting/index2.html

The Colored Canary Aviary- a great website with many helpful articles about nutrition, breeding, molting, etc. www.aaawebmaster.com/canary

Canary Lovers Webring- a ring of web sites devoted to canaries. www.o.webring.com/hub?ring=canary

Another website containing great articles about canary care- check out the canary cage recommendations! www.members.aol.com/PacificASC/ginger

Up At Six-an excellent source of avian related information. www.upatsix.com

A number of information sheets about topics such as trimming nails and vitamins. Mostly oriented to hookbills, but has some interesting content applicable to canaries as well. www.shell.pubnix.net/~mhagen/docu/infoshet.html

Frank's Fife Page- nice website about Fife canaries. Includes information about breeding cinnamon birds. www.geocities.com/Heartland/Fields/6270

Hans Classen's colored canary website- written entirely in German, but provides a wonderful gallery of photos of colored canaries. Worth taking the time to locate a translation program on the web, too! www.hansclassen.de

Bird Hobbyist- huge assortment of articles, links to organizations, etc. about all things avian www.birdhobbyist.com

Diseases and Conditions

Website about diseases and conditions, treatments and current research. Very in depth and informative. You can also locate a certified avian vet on this website. www.avianweb.com/diseases.htm

Species specific diseases and conditions- scroll down to canaries. Has links to research and articles related to conditions. www.avianweb.com/BirdSpeciesSyndroms.htm

A list of herbal and home remedies for birds. www.avianweb.com/homeremedies.htm

Ask-A-Vet - online answers and advice! www.askvetadvice.com

Cages, Supplies, and Other Bird Needs

Abba seed and myriad other products for birds. The company does not accept credit cards- they accept checks or money orders by mail order only. Sometimes Abba products are sold through local and online dealers- check the dealer list for a location near you or an online dealer. www.abbaseed.com

Inexpensive, no frills cages for breeders. www.birdbreedingcages.com

Company offering wide array of nutritional and health products as well as breeder supplies. www.birds2grow.com

Nice bird cages at reasonable prices. www.birdandcage.com

Custom built birdcages and flights. www.cornerslimited.com

Source for bulk quantities of bee pollen, spirulina and other supplements for birds- I have not found a less expensive source anywhere. They do offer trial shaker sizes if you need smaller amounts. www.bulkfoods.com

Cages and cage building supplies of all sorts. www.countryboycages.com

Bird food and some supplies. Family owned and operated, they sell seed in any amount and also custom mix seed. www.hermanbros-seed.com

New York Bird Supply- supplier of a wide assortment of seed brands, including Abba. www.nybird.com

Birdcare Company; sells such products such as vitamin and mineral supplements, specialty diets, probiotics, breeding and molting supplements. www.birdcareco.com

Sells bird food, supplements, and supplies by mail order. Offers Quiko products. www.orchidtreeexotics.net

Red Bird Products- in business since 1945, they offer a range of supplies for bird breeders. www.redbirdproducts.com

Offers a waterslager song CD which includes a helpful description of each of the notes. www.waterslager.com

Canary Clubs and Organizations
(some of these websites also provide articles on care, showing, etc.)

American Singer Club. www.upatsix.com/asc

Michigan chapter of the American Singer Club: DRAGON, Chapter 22. www.upatsix.com/asc/dragon.htm

American Waterslager Society. www.waterslagers.com

United Gloster Breeder's website- interesting breeding information applicable to all breeds, a no-egg nestling mix recipe and a nice article on breeding blue canaries. www.glosters-usa.com

Oakland International Roller Club- site also offers informational articles on breeding, feeding, etc. www.geocities.com/Heartland/8813

References

1. Linda Hogan, *Canary Tales*, 13th ed (1999)
2. Herman Osman, *Canary Breeding Tips and Tricks* (Chicago: Audubon, 1958)
3. Robert Stroud, *Stroud's Digest on the Diseases of Birds* (T.F.H. Publications, 1964)
4. G. B. R. Walker, *Colored, Type, and Song Canaries* (New York: Arco Publishing Company, 1977)
5. W. E. Brooks, *Guide to Canary Breeding and Exhibiting* (London: The Mitre Press)
6. G. T. Dodwell, *Encyclopedia of Canaries* (T.F.H. Publications, 1976)
7. Klaus Speicher, *Singing Canaries* (T.F.H. Publications, 1981)
8. American Singers Club, Inc., *Constitution, Bylaws, and Standards* (1992)
9. Nola Miller Fogg, *Encyclopedia of Canaries* (Chicago: Audubon, 1955)
10. Howard Fogg and Nola Miller Fogg, *Encyclopedia of Canaries and Other Cage Birds, 6th ed.* (Louisville: Audubon, 1942)
11. Claude St. John, *Canary Breeding For Beginners*, 16th ed. (London: Poultry World)
12. American Cage Bird Magazine, various issues
13. Gary A. Gallerstein, D.V.M., *The Complete Bird Owner's Handbook* (New York: Howell, 1994)
14. Mary L. Wulff-Tilford and Gregory L. Tilford, *All You Ever Wanted To Know About Herbs For Pets* (Irvine, CA: BowTie Press, 1999)
15. The Merck Veterinary Manual, 8th ed., ed. Susan E. Aiello, B.S., D.V.M., E.L.S. (Whitehouse Station: Merck & Co., 1998)
16. Birkhead, Tim, *A Brand New Bird- How Two Amateur Scientists Created The First Genetically Engineered Animal* (New York, Perseus Books Group, 2003)
17. Alberta Reidel, multiple conversations with author.
18. Jessie Durkin, multiple conversations with author.
19. Michael Grohman, multiple conversations with author.
20. Judy Snider, multiple conversations with author.
21. Ed Medrano, multiple conversations with author.
22. www.robirda.com.
23. Flock Talk archives- Robirda's archive of her biweekly eZine devoted to canaries and other small birds.